CAD Fundamentals
for Architecture

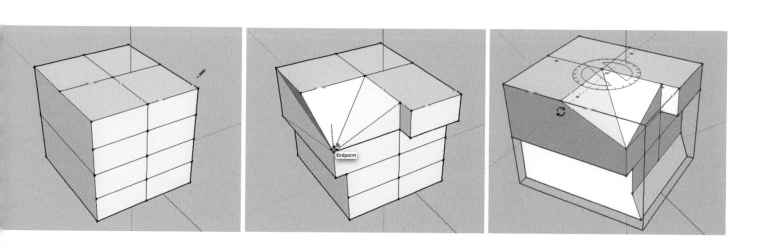

Published in 2013
by Laurence King Publishing Ltd
361–373 City Road
London EC1V 1LR
Tel +44 20 7841 6900
Fax +44 20 7841 6910
E enquiries@laurenceking.com
www.laurenceking.com

A catalogue record for this book is available from the British Library

ISBN 978 178067 282 3
Designed by John Round Design
Project Editor: Gaynor Sermon
Copy Editor: Angela Koo
Printed in China

CAD Fundamentals
for Architecture

ELYS JOHN

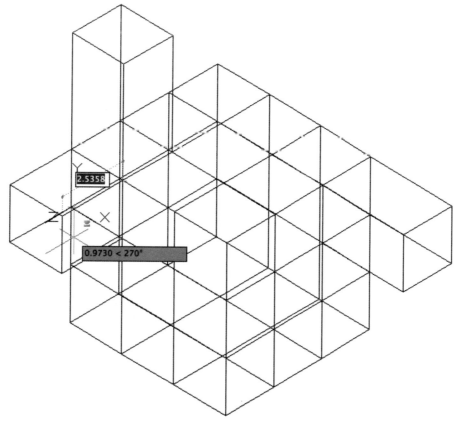

Laurence King Publishing

Contents

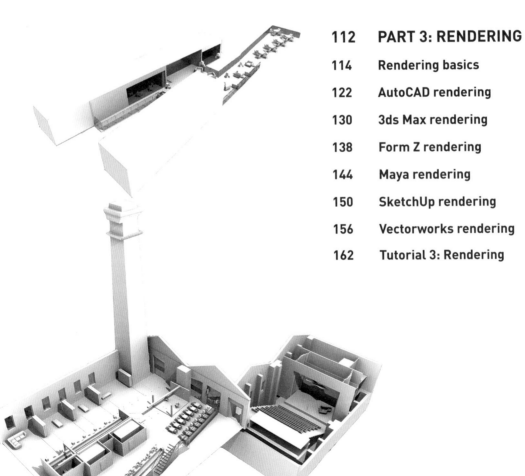

Related study material is available on the Laurence King website at
www.laurenceking.com

Introduction

Drawing is often referenced as a hand-rendered activity, and today it still plays an important creative role in the design development of architecture and interiors. Many architecture and design courses emphasize the importance of hand drawing and modelling as an effective way of communicating and developing a design brief but, while the role of hand drawing is undoubtedly a significant one, the reality of day-to-day design practice now places far more importance on drawing and modelling using digital means.

Increasingly, computer-aided-design, or CAD, is becoming the professional norm in terms of both creativity and efficiency, and this book examines the fundamentals of digital rendering for architects and students. There is a consistent formal language within CAD that references

key methods of drawing and modelling, and, by showing examples from a variety of software programs, this book can be used as a global reference rather than a guide to any one specific type of software.

The main aim of this book is to demystify 2D and 3D software interfaces and provide a detailed explanation of the key skills required in architectural design, from simple 2D drawing and 3D construction methods to more complex rendering techniques. The programs included are some of those most commonly used in education and in industry: SketchUp, Vectorworks, Form Z, AutoCAD, 3ds Max, Maya and Photoshop.

Different software programs are examined alongside each other, so that you can see how similar tasks are

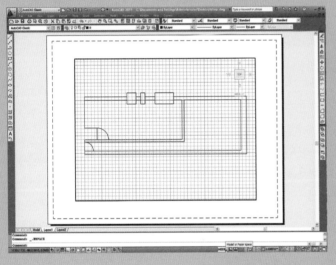
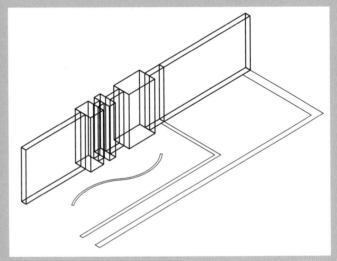
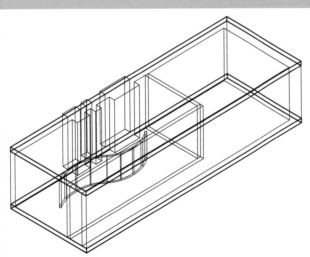
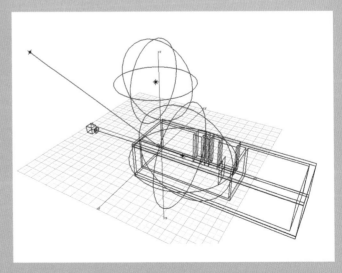

Chapters 1 and 2 guide you through the basics of 2D drawing and 3D modelling, while step-by-step tutorials take you through the process of creating a building from scratch.

performed across the range of programs. Step-by-step tutorials are included in each chapter, showing how to draw, model and render a building from start to finish using a variety of programs, and tip boxes provide further references to alternative software types. This will allow you to develop a broad awareness of what can be achieved with CAD and become less reliant on one specific software type, to become a global user.

In the final section, all of the skills demonstrated in the book are brought together to show the step-by-step rendering of an iconic architectural building – the Barcelona Pavilion. This demonstrates how the constituent parts of a project come together. There is also information on Building Information Modelling (BIM), which is fast becoming an integral part of architectural design and manufacture. A comprehensive resource section includes troubleshooting tips, a glossary, and suggestions for further reading as well as useful websites.

It is my hope that this book will assist architecture and interior design students as well as existing practitioners who are unfamiliar with CAD or whose skills are rusty. A common fault with some courses is the lack of formal CAD teaching; quite often students are left to it. This book offers a solid grounding in the fundamentals of CAD, and shows how to complete architectural visuals to a professional standard.

Chapters 3 and 4 show how to render a building and produce presentation visuals. Clear tutorials allow you to work through the process yourself.

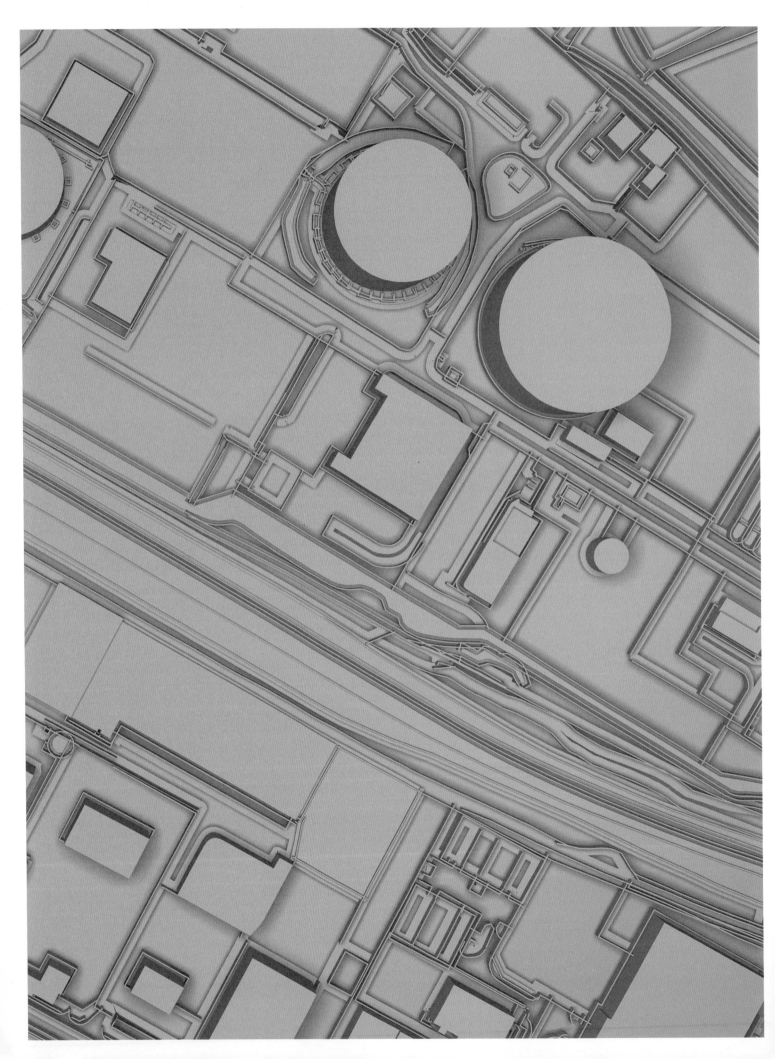

PART 1 2D DRAWING

INTRODUCING CAD

On first encounter the CAD interface can look daunting. Throughout this first section I will introduce a simple way of thinking about and using CAD packages. It may not be the quickest – there are always quicker ways to do things, although this comes with practise – but the following core principles relate more closely to traditional drawing board practice than they do to traditional CAD instruction. Relating back to drawing board practice is a key mindset to get into before you approach CAD drawing.

Below
This sectional perspective of the Atelier Bow Wow house (the practice's office) shows unprecedented orthographic detail. Visual rendering can provide the look of a scheme; drawing, and particularly this level of orthographic CAD drawing, can provide us with the ergonomic and construction information to rigorously illustrate the building.

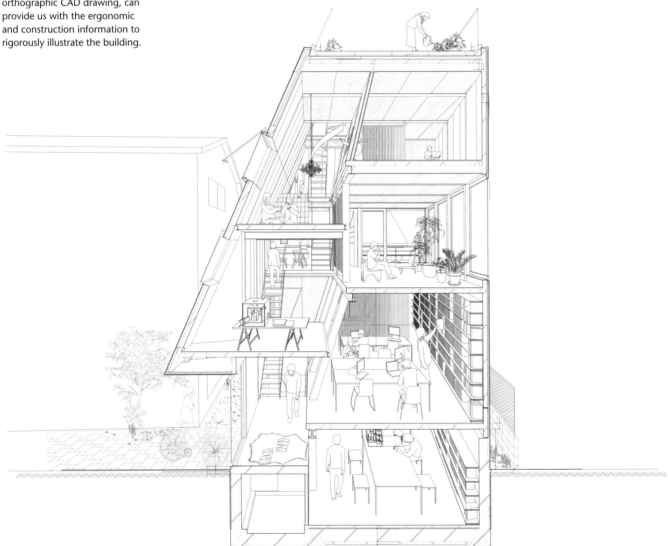

The drawing board

When we are presented with a drawing board we have a key set of drawing aids to use. The first is the board itself; this can be related to working space of the CAD program – the screen space. The obvious difference is the scale of things: drawing boards typically come in A3, A2, A1 or A0 size and you are required to work at a given scale when drawing – 1:100, 1:50, etc. The first issue to grasp within CAD programs is that the scale of the CAD environment is infinite; the CAD working space is not restricted by the dimensions of the drawing board. The first thing we can do, therefore, is discount the need to work at a specific scale, which frees us from making that decision until the drawing is completed.

The principle within the majority of CAD programs is to work at 1 unit = 1 architectural unit. In the UK 1 unit = 1mm, for Germany the units are metres, and for the USA the units are in American imperial. For all their differences, if you adopt the unit of your country you can easily transfer that into an infinite drawing board space in the CAD program.

Navigation

Navigation equates to the use of the eye and hand. Within drawing board practice you move the slide rule and the set square to navigate to the area of the drawing that you wish to develop. For CAD practice the same thing is performed through the movement and commands of the mouse.

Over recent years this ability to navigate around a drawing has been greatly improved and simplified through the development of multi mouse buttons. The almost universal introduction of the scroll wheel middle mouse button has helped simplify this process further. Within most CAD programs a press down on the middle scroll wheel allows you to pan (move the drawing to your desired area) which, along with a scroll of the same wheel, allows you to zoom in and out of that desired area. If we are again to relate this to traditional practice then it equates to the movement of the slide rule and set square to the desired area, while the zoom facility is the interaction of the eye/head to the area of the drawing you wish to focus on. Many people find that when initially using a CAD program they lose the drawing – a key tip is to take a step back to look and find the whole picture; in CAD terms this is universally done through the Zoom Extents command.

Drawing and drawing aids

It is possible to draw any shape or form with a pencil or pen – in most cases it is as quick as any CAD program. Indeed it is sometimes quicker to pick up a pencil than to turn on a computer and start up a CAD program!

When using a drawing board to draw there is a set of tools that you need before drawing commences:

- Drawing pencil – wooden, mechanical or wood-encased to create the line; technical pens to firm up the precision of drawing information.
- T-square or parallel rule to ensure a precise straight line; a set square or adjustable triangle to allow you to work in angular increments.
- A compass, to allow for drafting arcs and circles; circles and other geometric shapes can also be drawn with templates.
- French curves and flexible curves for drawing irregular curves.

With this core tool set you are able to draw anything – any shape, form or construction – and, as seen throughout architectural history, create complex building forms.

In CAD terms we can also create any drawn representation through a similar limited tool set. Software providers spend much time developing new tools and interfaces to speed up the process of drawing construction but if you can put this to one side, particularly as a novice user, you will gain a better understanding and overall competence in using CAD. As mentioned earlier, there are much more advanced methods of CAD construction but you should start by focusing on the competence of a similar tool set to that of drawing board practice.

ICON REFERENCES

The set square/orthographic and drawing aids

Top to bottom
throughout: AutoCAD;
SketchUp; Vectorworks

Drawing aids such as the set square and parallel rule are as important to CAD drawing as they are to traditional technical drawing. Unlike the drawing board these tools are not typically evident in the interface. They are present, quite often automated, as a way to provide the user with the option of drawing a straight line vertically or horizontally or even at polar increments. From the beginning it is important to familiarize yourself with the whereabouts of these tools.

Each software provider places them differently within the interface but they all provide the same functionality. You will also normally find Points Snap in the same location. This provides you with the ability to pick up a line at a given point from an existing drawn line. You will have the option to pick it up at an end point, midpoint or even a parallel point.

The line, the polyline

The Line is the primary drawing tool provided by CAD programs. In the case of AutoCAD there are many types of line provided: multiline, construction, parallel, etc. but for sheer adaptability the polyline stands out as the modern day equivalent of a pencil. It is an editable line – its thickness or shape can be altered and the line can be easily adapted to perform 3D operations. Other

CAD programs will use the Line tool. One of the major productivity savings of CAD compared to hand drawing is due to the fact that the Line tool becomes the pencil and pen operation. In the days of the drawing board you would construct in pencil and then trace over a final drawing in ink – a very time-consuming business.

The rectangle

Generally, when starting out I think using the rectangle tool is not particularly important. If we keep to the core basics of drawing board practice then most rectangle representations are easily constructed using the Line/Polyline tool. In drawing board practice, a rectangle template was useful for finer detailed representations, similar to circle templates.

The arc

The Arc tool equates to the compass. It allows you to draw a curved line of infinite radius. In drawing board practice this may have been constructed with the use of a compass, a beam compass for a larger radius, or even a French curve for more fluid arc arrangements. Within CAD the Arc is the tool of choice when creating curves because it typically gives you a three-point arc that can be manipulated through 'grips' to form a specific curve. This can then be used to form a door swing or an arched wall structure. When drawing arcs it is best (unlike for drawing board practice) to draw them in roughly and then move them into your desired shape or form. This is where the addition of grip editing supersedes the use of the drawing board. In drawing board practice you would spend

many hours constructing curves – indeed this was the most difficult thing to carry out when drawing by hand. Now with the provision of editable arcs (through grip editing) you are able to revisit and refine your curved lines. A welcome addition and practice for a novice is the ability to chain the arcs to form very complex variations of a single line. In practice it is always preferable to use multiple chained arcs to form a deviating arced line rather than using one of the other spline or free curve line tools provided by software developers.

The circle

The circle provides us with a complete compass tool. Where the arc provided us with an open curve, this creates a closed circle. The central point of the radius is typically the point where you would place the compass point, but in CAD terms the position of this can always be moved. In terms of editing it is quite a simple process to alter the radius or trim and cut the circle into an arc form.

Modify

As with drawing board construction, many of the lines you draw will be unwanted. Practices within hand drawing varied greatly and many ingenious ways of removing lines were employed – for the simple removal of a draft line a rubber would be used for pencil drawing; for inked drawings it became trickier and tools such as the erasing shield were used to protect the areas of the drawing that you did not want to be removed. There are two commands within the CAD environment that complement these actions.

First is simply the Erase/Delete command. In nearly all cases of CAD software this is as simple as selecting the desired line and looking for your Delete button; there is no need to search for an icon, as it is the simplest of commands to execute by keyboard. The second command is similar to that of the erasing shield and typically called 'trim'. It is a useful tool that helps you either tidy up unwanted lines as you go along or create more complex shapes from multiple line constructions.

Move/Copy

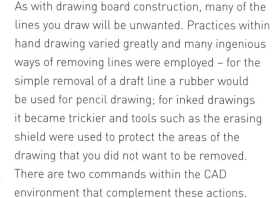

The Move tool is often bundled with the Copy tool and it allows you to move your chosen selection. The standard icon for Move is the compass symbol. Within AutoCAD you can simply activate the Move command by typing M and the Copy command by typing CO. One of the major advantages of CAD drawing over hand drawing is the computer's ability to replicate instantly. In the days of the drawing board one would trace and replicate a repeated part of a drawing – a laborious task that often resulted in less-than-satisfactory consistency. The Copy command has advanced greatly in recent years; it 'instinctively' lets you multi-copy rather than having to re-execute a command. As a beginner, it is important to keep executing the command so you get used to the copy interface of your chosen software. Take time to familiarize yourself with this basic operation.

Offset

Offset can be seen as an advancement of the Move/Copy tool. It allows you to specify a set distance and direction to copy or move an object or line to. It is particularly useful when constructing wall thickness or for the basic multi-copy of drawn information. There is another tool that automates this command into a more complex operation known as 'Array', but I would recommend that you use Offset as a beginner's tool. Once you have mastered that then you can experiment with array. Note that in SketchUp you can only offset a co-planar object, e.g. a rectangle or circle, known as a 'closed object'.

SUMMARY

Using a basic tool set available in all CAD programs you can construct any 2D drawing.
- **polyline** (line), **arc** and **circle** to create
- **trim, copy, move, offset** and **delete** for modification.

- Combined with a basic understanding of the navigational interface you will be well equipped to draw any 2D drawing CAD representation.
- The complexity of your drawing will rely not on the software you use, but the complexity of your design thinking.

SETTING UP A USER INTERFACE

The user interface is often referred to as the UI. Each manufacturer of CAD software has its own version, but there are common attributes between the different software types. The UI will often contain the navigation, drawing, modelling, rendering, annotation, modification, tool and properties palettes, etc. The most useful interface feature is the icon, as these will often indicate clearly the tool function. A text box explanation will pop up as you move your mouse across the icon. The majority of CAD software will also have a command line or script interface where specific commands or operations can be performed. CAD software developers continually upgrade their interfaces, and year-to-year you may find that the UI has changed. While these improvements are often helpful they can be equally frustrating, as you may need to search for some time to find a specific tool. However, even with the most radical of changes the fundamental operations/commands are usually executed in the same manner. The drawing setups in the following section are basic and relate to a typical UI setup. Whatever software you use, it can be beneficial to give yourself a few minutes to orientate yourself. In many cases you'll be able to customize the UI or set it to a preferable software version.

AutoCAD

AutoCAD's interface has developed from a command-based program to a command icon-led program. It was developed in line with DOS, the first Windows operating system.

Today there are three important user interfaces to work with. The latest generation is based on the ribbon format, an interface that is geared more towards a icon approach. AutoCAD Classic is a useful and timeless interface that is often favoured as it has been a familiar setup since release 14. A new interface recently introduced is the Mac version, which retains the same tool operations but has a very different interface to its Windows counterparts.

2D and annotation

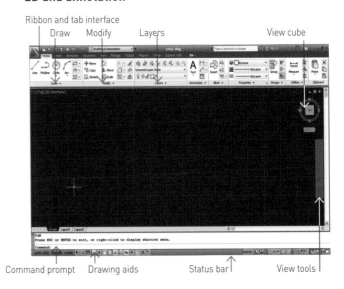

Ribbon and tab interface
Draw Modify Layers View cube
Command prompt Drawing aids Status bar View tools

AutoCAD Classic

Drop-down menu View tools Layers Layer properties View cube
Draw
Modify
Command prompt Drawing aids Status bar

AutoCAD MAC

Layers and properties
Drop-down menu View cube
Workspace select
Draw/Modify
Inquiry UCS
Command prompt Status bar View tools
Drawing aids

THE COMMAND PROMPT

The Command prompt is universally the most important element of the AutoCAD interface. It gives you the ability to type in any of AutoCAD's commands. There is no need to select the area, if you just type [when in command mode] it will activate the tool. Further sub levels of tool are also adjusted through this interface. AutoCAD has recently introduced a dynamic input method for this interface, where the keyboard entry occurs in the screen environment (right).

```
Command: _WSCURRENT
Enter new value for WSCURRENT

Command:
```
−15155.0849,2879.6422,0.0000

DRAWING LIMITS

You can use the LIMITS command prompt to set up the drawing limits of a drawing. If you have a building that is 5000mm x 5000mm you can use this function to set the MODEL drawing page to these limits, e.g. set the Model space to 6000, 6000.

```
Reset Model space limits:
Specify lower left corner or [ON/OFF]
```

When you reset the drawing view it will always return to the limits you have set. Introduced later is the Zoom/ Extents command which will also include everything drawn in the window. LIMITS is the equivalent of the page setup that you will create in SketchUp and Vectorworks.

TEMPLATES

You can start up AutoCAD and just begin drawing; that, in many ways, is the simplicity of the program. When used in architectural practice the practice will often have its own template to work with.

When you start AutoCAD it will be the ACAD template that is the default. Other templates are geared up for other environments such as 3D. In the workplace you may load a template that has a title box format, with company name and other drawing info. This is often in a template

Default ACAD template

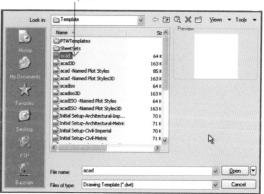

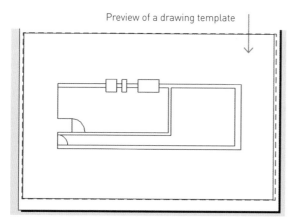

Preview of a drawing template

A typical AutoCAD drawing template with notes and title drawing block

Setting up the AutoCAD Interface

The default AutoCAD 2D drafting and annotation interface can look quite complex and you may wish to simplify it. We will go through this now. First, familiarize yourself with the drawing aids: Ortho is always based in the bottom left menu. This is the tool that equates to the set square and parallel motion. Also in this menu is another aid called 'Polar Tracking', which allows you to draw in polar increments. The Object Snap settings are also located here. These are the three drawing aids that you will use most often.

There is also a set of tools highlighted on the right. Combined with the middle mouse button zoom and pan feature, these provide your basic navigation tools.

While in command AutoCAD has many variables that can be used to alter the tool setup, but beware as it can be difficult to know how to reset a default configuration.

When the cursor has a square and crosshair present it is ready for a command

These are your Basic navigation tools. Your mouse is a key navigation tool

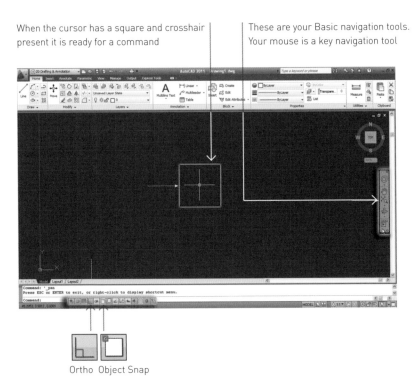

Ortho Object Snap

AUTOCAD CLASSIC WORKSPACE

In the bottom right-hand corner you will see a pop-up tab with 2D Drafting & Annotation written on it. This is the default start-up for 2011 but has been present in AutoCAD since Version 2007. Change that setting to AutoCAD Classic. The screen changes into its traditional look, giving you more screen and fewer icons.

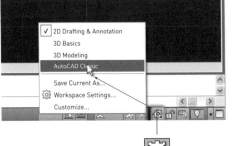

Menu shows AutoCAD workspaces:
2D Drafting and Annotation
3D Modelling
AutoCAD Classic (highlighted)

Workspace settings

CLEAN SCREEN WORKSPACE

Changing the user interface from AutoCAD Classic to Clean Screen will allow you to set up AutoCAD in its simplest form, cleaning the screen of all icons and any other distractions. If you change the settings you will find the lack of visual distractions beneficial for learning. However, if you want to go straight into the drawing task without using the following setup then simply proceed to the tutorial on page 24.

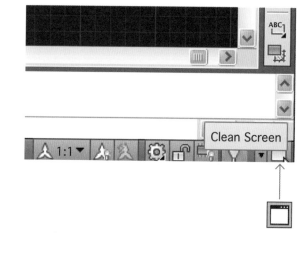

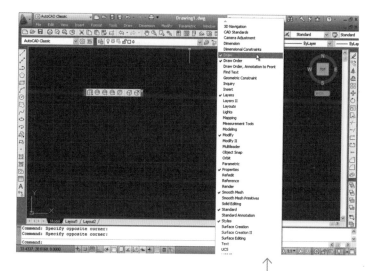

AutoCAD in Classic mode: right-click menus

TIP RIGHT-CLICK MENUS

AutoCAD Classic gives you right-click menu functionality from any of the icons present in the window. This functionality also exists in many other familiar programs, such as Microsoft Word. This is very useful as it allows you to find any icon groups (commands) quickly and easily.

AutoCAD in Clean Screen mode: keyboard entry.

TIP ESCAPE

A beginner will often try to execute a command when already in a Command mode, such as Polyline or Trim. Check that you have the Command prompt open. If not, you may press Escape to bring the square back up. Escape is a useful button for the beginner and does exactly what it says – lets you escape and try again.

SketchUp

SketchUp is the simplest interface you are likely to find in CAD software. It's because of its simplicity that most users find it very easy to navigate.

The drop-down menus contain most of SketchUp's commands. The basic tool set resides in the interface, known as the 'getting started', tool set it contains the fundamental tools needed to create a model. A further expanded tool set can be opened with the View › Toolbars menu. Additional format operations such as Styles, Materials, Layers and Scenes can be opened with the Windows menu.

The status bar will tell you what options are available for a command. You should read this as some of the options are useful and expand the tool base capabilities. The Measurements toolbar will give you numerical information, and you can also enter specific measurements in this field, such as the length of a line.

Google SketchUp is set up for a 3D modelling environment. In both 2D drawing and export terms it is preferable to set the view from the default Shaded view to Wireframe. The default Shaded view creates fields from any series of lines that create a closed object. This is particularly useful for the Presspull command that we will be using in the 3D modelling part of this book.

Having this feature activated while drawing a 2D drawing can be troublesome. In Wireframe mode you can focus on the drawing of lines rather than the creation of closed objects. Wireframe also relates the drawing environment to that being used in other programs – it sets you up in a 2D line environment. It also simplifies the export of the drawing as a line drawing.

This setup is comparable to that in AutoCAD. You won't be able to clean the screen or change the background colour, but as a free program this is quite impressive.

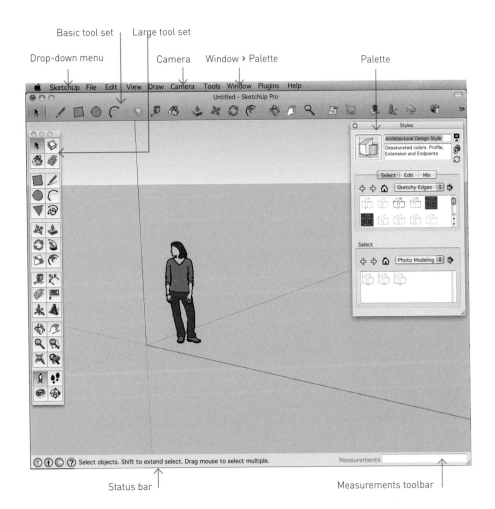

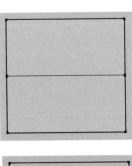

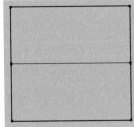

Top An example of a square in Shaded view; a field is created so it can easily be Presspulled in a 3D environment.

Below The same square in Wireframe mode. The shading is turned off as we want to be in a 2D drawing environment.

Vectorworks

Vectorworks has an expansive interface with many elements that will require a good understanding of CAD software to utilize. It's geared up for architectural drawing and annotation.

The pull-down menu contains most of the commands found in the interface and many other additional commands. In the toolbar area you will find a grouping of the most common drawing tools needed: Layers, Scale, Zoom, Working Planes and Views are all grouped in this area. There are many important palettes in the Windows › Palettes menu. Object info, Attributes, etc. allow you to modify existing drawn elements.

The basic tool set is the default, you can open the tool sets dialogue using the Windows › Toolsets option; this will give you 3D tools along with many more tool sets. Vectorworks uses the floating data bar to enter dimensional information, such as the length of a line or the angle of an object.

A drawing setup in Vectorworks is a fairly simple affair. When you start up the program it will ask you to select a template, such as Architect mm. To draw relative (direct line input) you need to set a scale to work with. The principle is similar to that you would adopt on a drawing board. Selecting the template defines a page size and a scale to work with. In the case of Architect mm the scale is set to 1:50 and the page size to American Letter. You can of course change both the scale and page size.

Finally, in keeping with the simple interface that we have set up in AutoCAD and the one provided with SketchUp, close any unneeded palette tabs to simplify the interface for this initial session. Leave the Tools, Snapping and Object Info palettes open as they will be useful. If you go to the Window menu you can easily reactivate all the palettes if you need to.

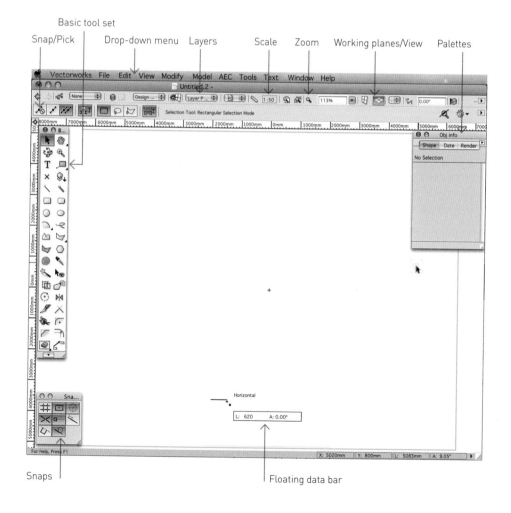

Basic tool set
Snap/Pick   Drop-down menu   Layers   Scale   Zoom   Working planes/View   Palettes

Snaps

Floating data bar

UNDERSTANDING LAYERS

The use of layers is a simple concept of organizing drawn and reference information. You will experience layers in most if not all digital creative programs.

Layers in CAD relate to the practice of overlaying drawings to provide increased levels of information, they provide you with the ability to switch and display the information, as you require it. With layers a drawing may not always be what it seems, it will often have many layers of additional information that you can access by turning the layers on and off. The ability to compose different types of information into different drawings, from one drawing file, is a very powerful organizational and data asset.

Layer organization: types and uses

2D and 3D layers You can use the layer system in most CAD programs to keep 2D and 3D work separated, so one layer could be for 2D linework then another for 3D solids.

Drawing and Annotation You can place dimensions and annotations on different layers, so you are able to hide the annotation and dimension layers so you can carry on drawing in objects. This is helpful, as too much linework can make a file difficult to work with.

Blocks Furniture and other spatial planning objects can be assigned to a specific layer. Quite often 3D models can be high res, which can really slow down a computer's performance. By putting them on their own layer you can hide them while working on the scheme and turn them on when you are ready to plot or render a scene.

Colour You can further identify specific groups of objects such as furniture, window frames, etc., by assigning them to a specific colour, so when you look at a CAD drawing you can quickly identify the elements. With reference to AutoCAD, in earlier versions (R.13 onwards) you had to assign colour to lineweights.

Lineweights/dotted lines With reference to AutoCAD: You can specify a lineweight or type to a layer. When making changes to lineweights or dotted lines it can be beneficial to place them on an individual layer so you can make quick amendments to a line type.

TIP ACTIVE LAYERS

If there is one thing to remember when using any program that has a layer interface, make sure that layer is active when you create an item or it will end up on the wrong layer, something I am personally guilty of to this day!

Below is an exploded drawing of a typical layer stack.

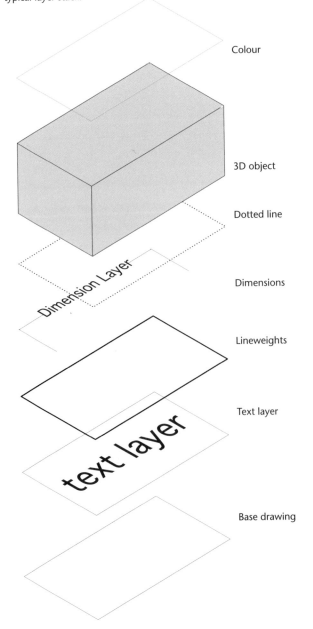

Colour

3D object

Dotted line

Dimension Layer

Dimensions

Lineweights

Text layer

text layer

Base drawing

Drawing organization

When you are working on plans of a building that has many floors, it can be very useful to overlay them on top of each other to check for consistency and alignments. If the plans are organized into layers you can quickly switch between each floor plane.

Move It can be difficult to move a complex object, especially if it is made up of ungrouped lines. You can use the Layer option to place all the related geometry on its own layer.

Material You can use layers to organize materials or textures.

Layer Groups You can further develop the density of the layer information by creating a Layer Group, a group of common layers; for example, all of the furniture in the scheme may be placed in a layer group

External references

External reference files, or Xref files as they are known in AutoCAD, are files that are imported into a drawing as a reference or as shared information. They can be brought in on a separate layer and then switched off when you have finished using them or switched on when you need to plot a final drawing.

One example would be the import of an image file of a plan to trace the linework as a CAD drawing. You would be able to alter the drawing at source with Photoshop, but when in the CAD environment it would be a uneditable reference [apart from basic modify commands such as Scale].

A typical Xref file in AutoCAD would be a common drawing detail or a drawing template with notes that would be used as a block and be common to multiple drawings. Any edit of this block or reference would be carried through to every drawing that contained that reference, therefore making the update of common drawing data more efficient.

Note: often with reference files they are not embedded in the actual file, they are a reference to the location of the file, a path to where the file is kept. You may need to keep a folder with the reference file as well as your working file.

> **TIP** REASSIGN LAYERS
>
> If you end up drawing an object on the incorrect layer you can use the match properties in AutoCAD or the eyedropper tool in other software programs to reassign the object to the correct layer.

AutoCAD Xref example. The reference drawing is shown in grey to indicate that it is a reference.

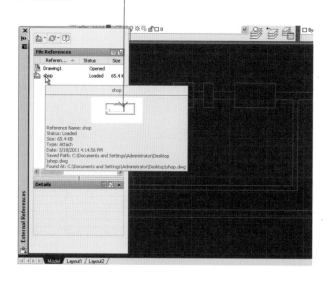

AutoCAD

AutoCAD has an extensive layers capability; it binds all of the assets into the Layers panel. The Layer Properties Manger contains all the elements and layer controls used in AutoCAD. As with Most AutoCAD tools it can be opened in multiple ways.

Ribbon: Home tab › Layers panel › Layer Properties Manager
Menu: Format › Layer
Toolbar: Layer
Command Line: LAYER
Layer Manager: The menu icon

When Drawing and creating layers you can often have empty layers or drawing fragments. These can be fixed via the command line:

PURGE. Purging your drawings gets rid of unused layers, annotation styles, blocks, etc.
OVERKILL Overkill removes redundant or overlapping geometry, such as 2 rectangles overlaid on each other or excessive points in a polyline.
Both commands used regularly will help keep your file size down and help you keep healthy file not over loaded with layers or duplicate objects

LAYER MANAGER FIELDS

① Active layer [green tick]
② On/off
③ Freeze
④ Lock [to stop any alterations to that layer]
⑤ Colour
⑥ Linetype [continuous or dotted}
⑦ Lineweight
⑧ Transparency
⑨ Plot Style [Colour 7 is the default pen for black]
⑩ Plot [If Plot Off is selected it will not plot the information or linework on that layer]
⑪ New Viewport Freeze [when in a viewport you can freeze the display of the layer in the viewport but it will still display in model space]

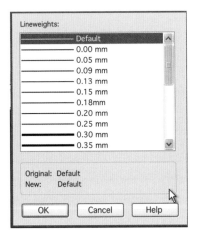

The lineweight pop-up dialogue. Most of the options are activated by a double click

Below: A typical layer setup for AutoCAD Illustration.

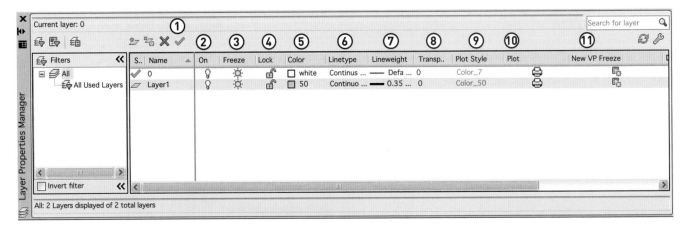

Vectorworks

Vectorworks uses a design layer system to keep all the drawn design information organized. Another layer level called Classes organizes line scale, line colour, etc. The Dimensions Layer Options [all dimensions are drawn on this Class as default] is also based in the Classes layer.

DESIGN LAYERS

① Visibility options: visible, invisible, grey [linework inactive but grey visible]

② Layer active [tick]

③ Design layer name

④ Stacking order [in front, behind]

⑤ Scale

⑥ Colour

⑦ Opacity [useful for images]

⑧ Background [Renderworks background]

CLASSES LAYER

You can create new classes and set the lineweight: every line you create while that classes is active will be placed in that Classes layer.

① Visibility options: Visible, invisible, grey [linework inactive but grey visible]

② Layer active [tick]

③ Class name

④ Use [yes or no]

⑤ Fill

⑥ Pen

⑦ Line [e.g. continuous or dotted]

⑧ Thickness

⑨ Marker [e.g. endcaps]

⑩ Texture [material]

DESIGN LAYER

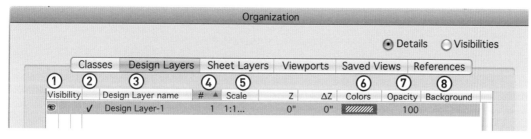

CLASSES LAYER

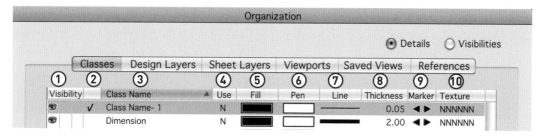

SketchUp

SketchUp's layer options are limited, but simple to use. Layer palette options provide you with visibility and colour. While it is a simple interface, you can still use the layer function to organize your work effectively.

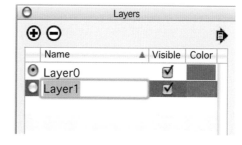

TUTORIAL 1 BASIC DRAWING EXERCISE

This exercise will introduce the key tools that were discussed in the Introduction. It is primarily an AutoCAD exercise but it can be applied to other programs such as Vectorworks and SketchUp too, since it deals with core tools that are available within all 2D drafting programs. The exercise will introduce these tools one at a time. When you feel you have gained enough confidence to move on to the next stage do so, but do not be reluctant to repeat any sections – doing so will help you to master the individual commands. This is an exercise that should be repeated as many times as necessary to build your skills.

You are going to use the command line for all sections of the exercise, as there are now no icons present. To relate this exercise to Vectorworks and SketchUp you will use the keyboard too, but since these interfaces do not have a command line interface you will use keyboard shortcuts. For this initial task I suggest you use the keyboard; you may well then choose to try the same exercise again using an icon-based approach.

The exercise is based on AutoCAD and you will see subheadings that relate each task to Vectorworks and SketchUp. As you will see, the software has little relevance; it is the mastery of the core set of tools that is important.

TIP SAVE YOUR WORK!

From this point on you should remember to save your file regularly as you work. Native file type suffixes are:
AutoCAD: .dwg
SketchUp: skp
Vectorworks: vwx

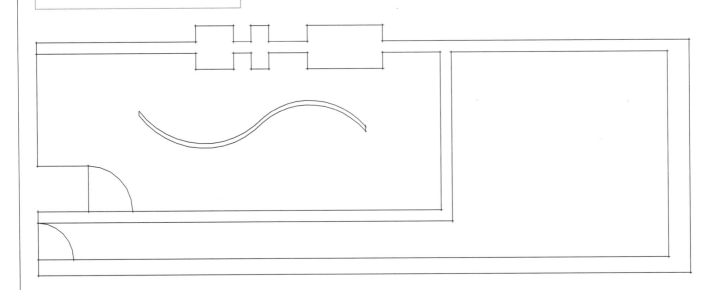

POLY/LINE TOOL

Draw the lines as shown in the diagram below. Note that dimension lines should be drawn lighter than or in a different colour to the main plan lines.

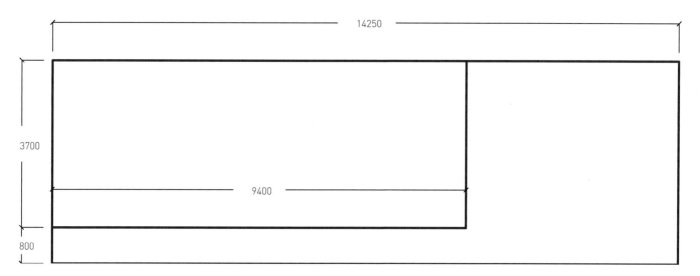

AutoCAD
Check to see that Ortho and End Snaps are activated.
→ Type in PL (polyline) on your keyboard
→ Click anywhere on the screen and use the mouse to indicate the direction you want it to go
→ Enter the line measurement (14250)

NOTE: It is good practice to take your hand off the mouse when entering a measurement. After entering the line measurement press Enter.

SketchUp
→ Type in L to activate the Line tool
→ Click anywhere on the screen and use your mouse to show the direction you wish the line to go in
→ Enter the line length with your keyboard; press Enter to confirm the distance (14250)
→ Escape to finish using the Line tool

Vectorworks
→ Type in 2 to activate the Line tool
→ Click in the far left-hand corner of the screen and use your mouse to show the direction you wish the line to go in
→ Enter the length of the line (14250)
→ Press Enter to complete the line

Use the Shift key to activate Ortho mode. Use the Tab key to move through the floating toolbar fields.

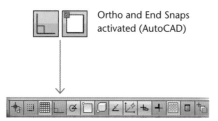

Ortho and End Snaps activated (AutoCAD)

TIP THE ENTER KEY

You can easily reactivate a command without retyping by pressing the Enter key on the keyboard after you have completed the command. Pressing Enter can terminate a line or, alternatively, you can just right-click on the mouse.

ZOOM/EXTENTS

You will notice that you will not see the end of the line, as the drawing limits have not been set. An easy way to set these limits is to use the Zoom/Extents command.

Your line will now fit the page. Scroll the wheel of the middle mouse button to zoom out further and press it down to pan around the drawing.

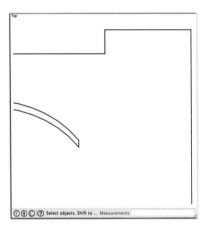

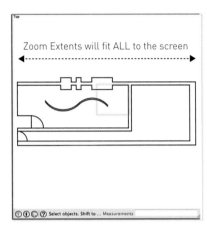

Zoom Extents will fit ALL to the screen

AutoCAD
→ Type in Z (zoom)
→ Press Enter
→ Type in E (extents)
→ Press Enter to confirm the command

SketchUp
Zoom/Extents
→ Shift + Z

It can also be found in Camera › Zoom Extents

Vectorworks
Use Fit to Objects rather than Zoom/Extents to fit the line to the page.
→ Cmd + 6 (mac)
→ Ctrl + 6 (pc)

NAVIGATION

The middle mouse button is key for effective drawing navigation. You should always use a mouse rather than a trackpad.
→ Scroll the middle mouse button to zoom in and out
→ Hold the middle mouse button down to pan (move a drawing around the window)

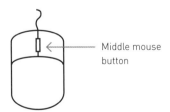

Middle mouse button

OFFSET/INWARDS AND OUTWARDS

Use the Offset tool to perform the three offsets shown below.

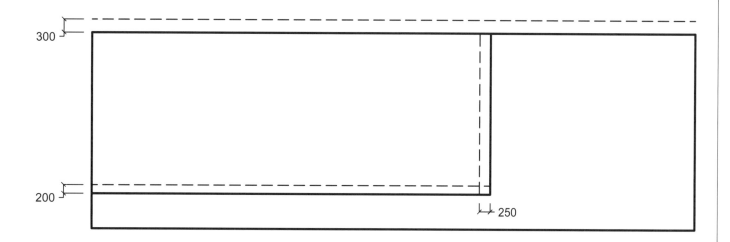

AutoCAD

AutoCAD = O (offset)

→ Type in O to activate the Offset command and press Enter.
  You will be asked for a distance to offset the line by. This can be entered on the keypad or specified by using the mouse.

→ Press Enter to confirm the distance; a small rectangle will appear

→ Select the line you wish to offset and click in the direction you wish to go in

You can select more than one line to offset as long as they all need to be offset in the same direction.

SketchUp

SketchUp = Alt (mac)/Ctrl (pc) + M
You cannot use the Offset tool to offset a singular line in SketchUp: you need to use the Move tool to Move/Copy.

→ Type M on the keyboard to activate the Move tool

→ Hold the Alt (mac)/Ctrl (pc) key to activate the Copy mode

→ Select the line to offset and use the mouse to indicate the direction

→ Type in the distance

→ The line will snap to the given measurement, in the direction you choose

Remove your hand from the mouse once you have shown the direction and make sure the Alt/Ctrl key is selected. Zoom in to select a copy by midpoint.

Vectorworks

Vectorworks = Shift + (hyphen)
Select a line/lines to offset and then select the Hyphen key while holding the Shift button to activate Offset mode.

→ It can often be simpler to use the icon to activate the tool

→ Select a line to offset

→ Enter the distance in the menu bar

→ Click on the screen to indicate the direction you want

Use the Cmd key (Mac) or Ctrl (PC) to select an object. A double click on most icons will bring up more icon preferences.

BASIC DRAWING EXERCISE /CONTINUED

POLY/LINE AND **OFFSET** TOGETHER

Draw the additional lines as shown below.
Draw in a line in the top left-hand corner using your snaps
offset along the given dimensions.

 Offset line in this direction

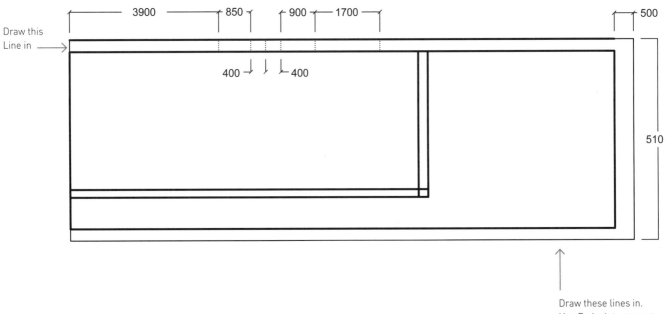

Draw this
Line in →

3900   850   900   1700   500

400 ↓ ↓ L 400

510

Draw these lines in.
Use Endpoints snaps to
draw the lines without
dimensions

TIP AUTOCAD

When the square icon appears you can
select multiple objects by a select sweep
from right to left; a green window will
appear as you do this.

MOVE/COPY COMMAND

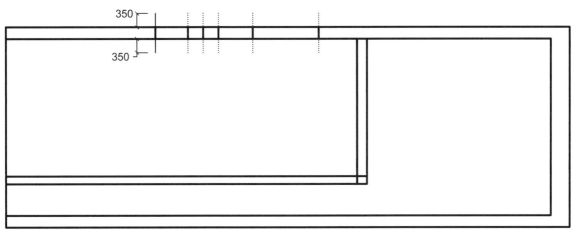

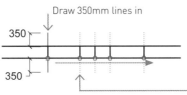

Draw 350mm lines in

Using the relevant copy command, pick up the lines at this point and drop them off at the points shown

 AutoCAD = M (move)

 AutoCAD = CO (copy)

 SketchUp = M (Move)

 SketchUp = Alt (mac)/Ctrl (pc) + M

 Vectorworks = X (selection)

 Vectorworks = 2 (line)

AutoCAD

Move: Draw the two 350mm lines as indicated, then activate the Move command by typing M and pressing Enter.

→ A small square will appear; use this to select the lines (multiple select) and press Enter

→ Pick the lines up at the shown point and move to the next row

→ Press Enter to finish with the tool

Copy: Activate the Copy command by typing in CO and then Enter.

→ Select the two drawn lines and press Enter

→ Pick them both up at the same point and drop them off repeatedly, as shown above

SketchUp

Draw the two lines as indicated. You need to preselect your lines using the Pick tool (Shift to add to a selection).

→ Type in M to activate the Move tool

→ Use the Alt (mac)/Ctrl (pc) key to perform the Copy command

Vectorworks

Draw the two lines as indicated. The Move/Copy command is performed through the 2D selection tool. Enter X on the keyboard.

→ Select the lines to move

→ To perform a copy press the Alt (mac)/Ctrl (pc) key to activate the Copy mode

---

TIP PICKING POINTS

In all cases you need to pick the items up at a specific point, since this has a relationship to where you want to drop them off. This skill/judgement is important when using all CAD software.

Endpoint

DELETE COMMAND

Select and delete the indicated line using the Delete button
on your keyboard. Continue to draw the missing lines as
shown below.

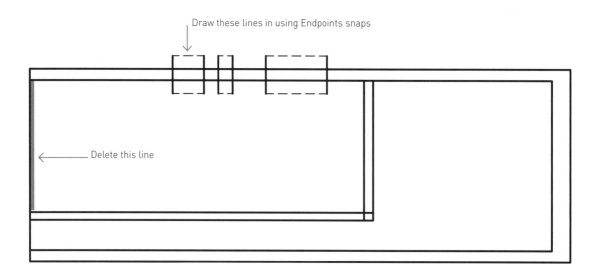

Draw these lines in using Endpoints snaps

Delete this line

DELETE

In CAD software there are various
icons that represent the Delete
command, but universally the
simplest way to delete an object is by
using the Delete keyboard key.

TIP SHIFT KEY

Most CAD software will let you add extra
objects to a pick command by using the
Shift key.

TIP GO BACK

You can always press Cmd + Z (mac) or
Ctrl + Z (pc) to go one step back.

Continue to draw the missing lines, as indicated below.

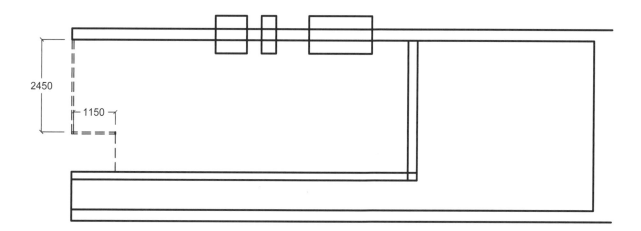

LAYER ORGANIZATION

Layers are really useful to group items (see 20)

AutoCAD

AutoCAD has a drop-down menu so that you can select which layer you want to work on. The Layers Properties dialogue can be opened by selecting the Stack icon.

Within the Layers Properties window you can adjust and add layers to the drawing. Line colour, lineweight, type, etc. can also be altered to be the default of that layer.

Vectorworks

Vectorworks follows the same format as AutoCAD. The palette can be opened by selecting the Stack icon next to the Layers drop-down.

Stack icon

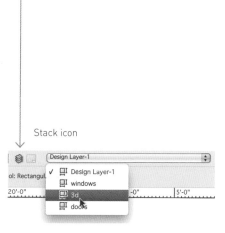

SketchUp

SketchUp has a very simple system of layers. They can be added by using the plus sign and chosen by selecting the layer's name. The palette is opened in the window's drop-down.

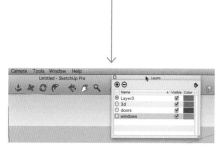

CIRCLE TOOL

Draw in the two circles as shown below.

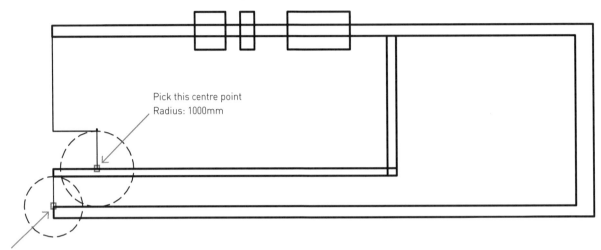

Pick this centre point
Radius: 1000mm

Pick this centre point
Radius: 800mm

AutoCAD
AutoCAD = C (circle)

→ Type in C (circle) and press Enter

→ Select the centre point of the circle at the points indicated in the diagram; press Enter

→ Specify the radii as indicated in diagram; press Enter

→ Reactivate the tool using the Enter button rather than re-entering the C command

SketchUp
SketchUp = C (circle)

→ Type in 6 to activate the Circle command; select the centre point of the circle

→ Use the Tab key to enter the radius; press Enter

Vectorworks
Vectorworks = 6 (circle)

→ Type in C

→ Select the centre point and type in the radius; press Enter to confirm

→ The tool will remain activated for the second circle

TRIM TOOL

The drawing is nearly complete. Now we need to tidy up
the unwanted and crossing lines used in its construction.
Follow the diagram below and delete the unwanted lines.

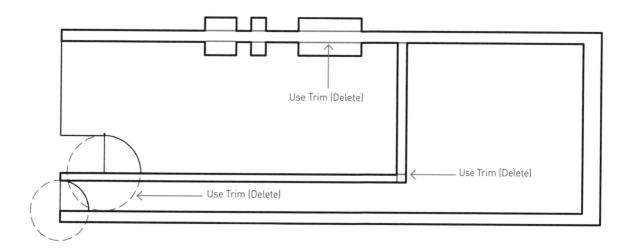

AutoCAD
AutoCAD = TR (trim)
→ Type in TR (trim) and press Enter;
   a small pick box will appear

You can then pick the individual lines
you wish to trim or, preferably, select
the whole drawing by a (click and
drag) select sweep from right to left;
a green window will appear as you
do this. Press Enter to confirm your
selection.
You will then be able to trim. Don't
forget to trim your circles to create
the door openings.

SketchUp
SketchUp = Spacebar (Delete key +
intersection)
There is no 'trim' command to
speak of. The trim command can
be completed using the Select tool
(spacebar)
→ Pick up an intersection/crossing
   line and press the Delete button

Vectorworks
Vectorworks = Alt + Shift + L (mac) /
Option + Shift + L (pc)
→ Press Alt + Shift +L/Option + Shift
   + L to activate the Trim tool
→ Select the lines that you wish
   to trim

TIP DELETE COMMAND

The lines must be crossing to perform
a trim – it needs a cutting edge. If you
cannot trim a line then the Delete
command will delete it. If you trim a
line by accident you can go one step
backwards in Trim by using the Cmd + Z
(mac)/Ctrl + Z (pc) command.

THE ARC

The final stage is to create a curved object within the building shell. The curve does not have to match the one shown here; this would be quite difficult to reproduce accurately. The main point is just to practise with the fluidity of a curved line – to experiment rather than replicate.

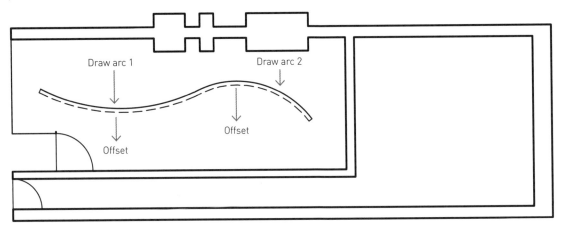

Draw arc 1

Draw arc 2

Offset

Offset

AutoCAD
AutoCAD = A (arc)
→ Type in A and press Enter

→ Draw in two curves anywhere within the building outline. The Arc tool requires three points to create a curve. Use Enter to reactivate the tool and draw in a second curve.

When you have drawn the curves ensure the command line is in Command mode (no tool selected) and click on the curves. This will bring up the 'grip edits'. Select the various grips individually and move them around to create a more flowing line. When you are happy, use Offset to give the object thickness.

SketchUp
SketchUp = A (arc)
Type in A (arc) and draw two three-point arcs anywhere on the screen
→ Type in M to select the Move tool and move over the arc entity

→ Select a midpoint or endpoint to grip edit

→ Click and hold to modify the arc

When happy with the curved lines connection perform a Copy/Offset.
→ Copy/Offset using the Move tool + Alt (mac) /Ctrl (pc) key

→ Enter in the distance you wish to copy using the Tab key

Vectorworks
Vectorworks = 3 (arc)
Arcs in Vectorworks are tricky; the grips are not as fluid as they are in other programs, so this will take time to master.
→ Type 3 and draw in two three-point arcs anywhere on the screen

→ Use the 2D Selection tool to edit the grips

Finish with a Copy/Offset command.

TIP SNAPS AND ORTHO

When drawing an arc and grip editing it is sometimes easier to turn off Snaps and Ortho.

GRIP EDITS

Grip edits are a way of modifying a shape's properties. They allow you to sketch in any shape and then alter its geometry. There is no tool as such that performs a grip edit – it is normally executed by invoking the grips when picking up an object.

The screenshots on this page illustrate the variations possible with grip edits. You will notice that for an arc there are endpoints, a midpoint and a centre grip. These can all be used to alter the arc form.

Draw the arcs anywhere in the window and use the grips to move the arc into place.

AutoCAD Select when the crosshair is in Command mode then drag into position.

The crosshair in Command mode. (Press Escape if you want to get out of a tool.)

SketchUp Select and drag using the Move tool.
You also use the Move tool for the offset.

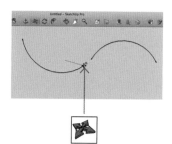

Vectorworks Experiment with the type of arc you create.

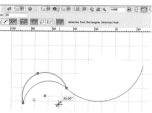

Select and modify using the Select tool.

TIP GRIP EDITS

You can also alter the length of a line, rectangular shape, circle, etc. using a grip edit. This can save you the trouble of redrawing an entity.
   It is sometimes easier to draw in a shape such as an arc in free space and then use grip edits to refine it.

Your finished drawing should look like the one shown below. If it does not then repeat the exercise until you build up some confidence with the tools that have been introduced so far.

DID YOU SAVE YOUR WORK AS YOU WENT ALONG?

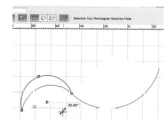

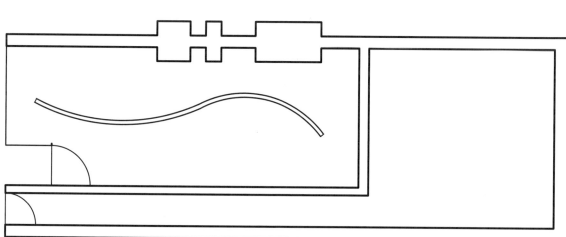

PLAN EXPORT/PRESENTATION DRAWING

Basic plan export

If you do wish to export the model into another program the universally suitable drawing format for programs is likely to be DWG. This is a suitable format for 3ds Max, Maya, SolidWorks, etc.

- AutoCAD: the native format for AutoCAD is DWG so there is little more to do than save the file to a suitable place.
- SketchUp: the free version of SketchUp only allows you to save the file in .skp (SketchUp format) but the Pro version will allow you to save (and import) the DWG format.
- Vectorworks: allows you to export the 2D drawing as a DWG format. If you have set up a 3D model it also allows you to export in various 3D modelling formats, such as 3ds Max.

In theory the export from one program to another should be a simple process. In reality it can be quite a buggy operation, with only some information being translated, or whole plans disappearing all together. Certain programs such as AutoCAD and 3ds Max naturally work together as the same software provider (Autodesk) produces them.

If you do intend to move from either SketchUp or Vectorworks into a different 3D program such as 3ds Max or Maya, it is best to try an export while you are still in Plan mode and complete the 3D modelling in that program. If you have completed a 3D final model and the export is flawed then there is a lot to lose.

Presentation drawing

The following categories are the basic requirements for effectively annotating a plan: lineweights, dotted lines, dimensions and text.

- Lineweights are not only aesthetically preferable, but they also provide a visual reference, express where a cut has taken place on a plan, and help the person reading a plan to judge spatial depth and solid structure.
- Dotted lines help show an object that is hidden or is above the plan cut.
- Dimensions are there to help measure a drawing that is not printed to scale.
- Text is essential for labelling entrances, room types, and so on; it should also be used to indicate the type of drawing, e.g. 'long section'.

In presentation terms CAD drawings are often devoid of any variation in lineweights; with the default .25 lineweight becoming predominant. It is important to use the lineweight functionality in your CAD program.

Export compatibility

Vectorworks: exchange of drawings in 2D and 3D between AutoCAD and Vectorworks is generally good.

SketchUp: this can be problematic and data may get lost. The way SketchUp works with surfaces rather than true solids causes issues, where objects are not true solids.

AutoCAD to SketchUp: there is a good chance you will lose any 3D information; 2D import of plans etc. is a little more successful.

SketchUp to AutoCAD: Will bring in boxes, walls, etc. as surface objects rather than true solids.

Do a simple test before importing your work: draw a box and try an import to check compatibility between software.

TIP IMPORT/EXPORT

All programs will allow you to export a file through the menu: File › Export. You may also select File › Import through the same menu tab.

Typical presentation drawing by
a student, showing a plan and
elevation.

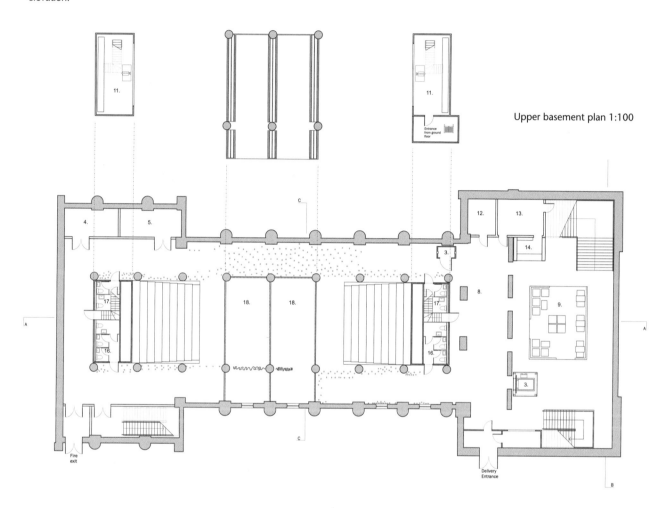

Upper basement plan 1:100

Basement plan 1:100

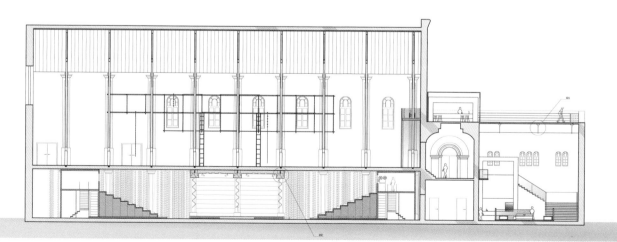

AutoCAD

ANNOTATION

Creating line thickness, dotted lines, dimensions and correctly proportioned text can initially be quite a time-consuming process. In AutoCAD it can appear very complicated – indeed it is! There are two spaces in AutoCAD. One is called Model space, and this is what we have used so far. The other space is called Paperspace; this is where you would traditionally lay out your drawings. Most of the tools of annotation are set up for use in Paperspace rather than Model space.

To keep things simple the annotation tools introduced are formatted for Model space – so you can carry on working in this space. This is primarily because we intend to export the drawing as a PDF and use Photoshop to set the final layout.

Model space/Paperspace

→ Model space is a environment where your drawing is in infinite space and your drawing units are typically 1 unit to 1 mm. It also comes with the AutoCAD trademark black screen.

→ Paperspace is typically set to a paper size, for example, A3 or A1. Within Paperspace you import viewports of your model – they can be set to plan (top), isometric or any view you choose. You then scale the view to so that it is appropriate for the paper size, e.g. 1:50. You can also annotate the paper with text, title boxes and so on.

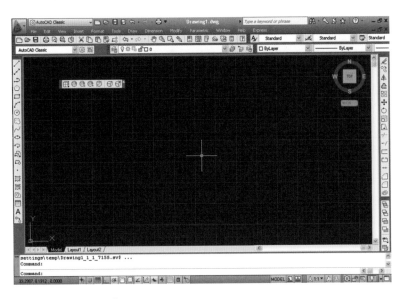

Typical Model space environment

The Model space tab selected

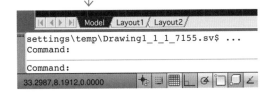

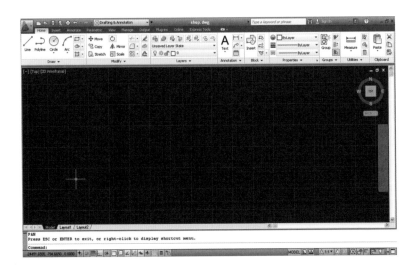

Typical Paperspace environment

The Layout tab selected

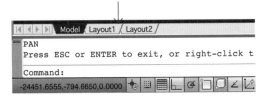

TIP PAPER VS MODEL

Paperspace can appear complicated. As a beginner it's best to stick to Model space – you can get the same results.

SETTING UP A
PAPERSPACE LAYOUT

You will need to set up your layout as the default will not be to a scale and will be in a default paper size.

Page setup

Right click on the Layout tab and select the Page Setup Manager; this will list the layouts in your file. Select the Modify button to edit the layout parameters.

Layout list

Modify layout

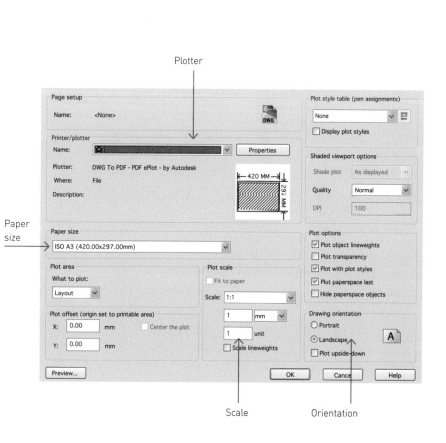

Page Setup Manager

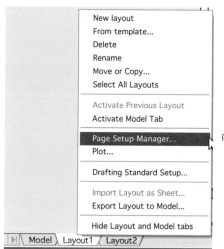

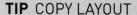

The page setup dialogue is very similar to the Plot/Print dialogue. Here you can set the plotter, paper size and the orientation of the page. The scale will typically be set to 1:1 as the drawing will be scaled in paperspace. Once the settings are made they are saved ready for plotting.

Plotter

Paper size

Scale

Orientation

TIP COPY LAYOUT

One you have created a layout you can copy it by right clicking on the layout tab and using the Move or Copy option.

Layout Paperspace

When you have selected and formatted your paper you will also need to formant the Viewport contained in the layout. By default there is a single viewport, the layout may contain as many viewports as you require, you can set the view ports to different views such as top or iso view.

You can use the View → Viewports to add extra viewports or create other layouts

DRAWING FORMAT

You can alter the scale and view of the viewport when you are in layout/model space. You activate this my toggling the tab labelled Paper or Model in the status bar. This can appear confusing initially as you will be used to Model space being in the black environment. By selecting Model in Layout mode you will have a link to the model in Model space.

In Layout Model space you can set the scale, change the model view and position the drawing. You will know you are in Model space as the viewport will be outlined with a black box.

In Paperspace Layout mode you can resize the viewport, add additional viewports, further annotation such as text and dotted lines.

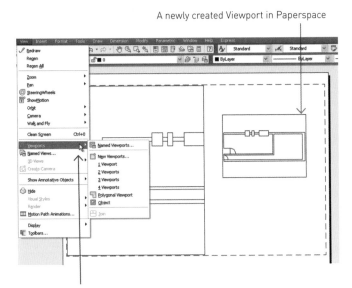

A newly created Viewport in Paperspace

AUTOCAD CLASSIC

The right click functionality of AutoCAD classic will allow you to use the useful Viewports toolbar

Viewport options   Set scale

Model tab   Scale option

Model Layout with black surround

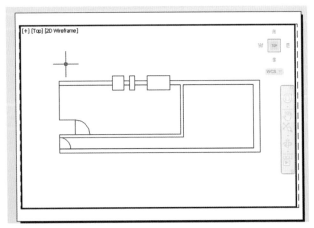

Paper Layout

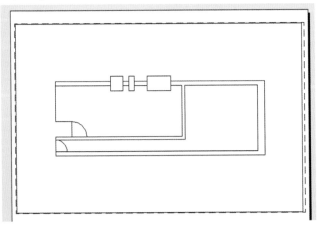

FORMATTING MODEL SPACE

The Lineweight dialogue is quite simple.
It's also a useful place to start any annotation
activity as it takes place in Model space. You can
preselect the lineweight before you draw the line
or, as I prefer, you can select a line and then
use the drop-down tab to specify the lineweight.

① Select the line in Command
mode so the blue grips appear

② Pick the lineweight from the
drop-down menu

③ Escape to come out of selection

This is the Properties menu bar

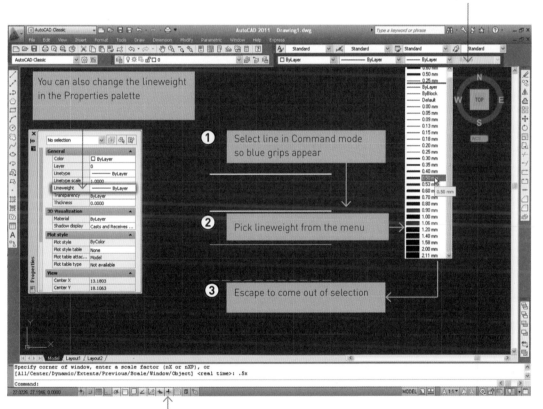

Show lineweights

NOTE: If you see no change in lineweight
then the icon is off (grey off/blue on). You
need to ensure the Show Lineweights
dialogue is turned on.

TIP LINEWEIGHT

The Properties tab can be opened by
double-clicking an object or a right
click and select Properties. If a line is
refusing to change weight or missing
bits out, just trace over it with the
Polyline tool and then select that line for
applying the weight.

DIMENSIONS, TEXT AND DOTTED LINES

These all work in a similar way – in Model space they are
nearly always subject to scale issues. They are initially
formatted for Paperspace so we have to tweak the scale
settings for the dotted line or text to be visible in Model
space. If you alter the scale of a dotted line in Model space
it may no longer display correctly in Paperspace.

The screengrab below shows you where dimensions,
dotted lines and text are located within the classic
AutoCAD interface.

TIP ZOOM TOOL

It's easy to lose a text object if you have
not entered in the correct text size.
Remember where you placed it and
use the Zoom tool to find it again.

Dimensions are selected from the menu bar or the
Dimension toolbar. Select the appropriate tool – Linear
is the simplest to use.

Dotted lines can be selected from the Properties palette.
Dotted lines are not loaded by default – you need to load them
through the Other option. Remember to select a line.

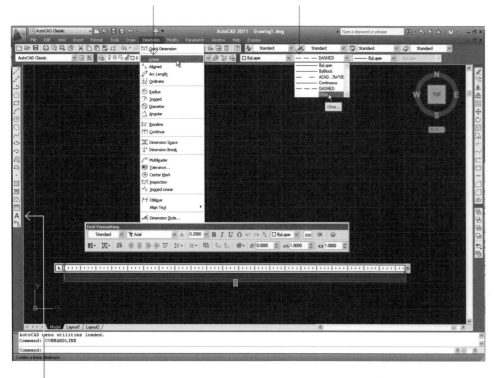

Text is selected from the Draw toolbar. Text is formatted for
Paperspace but you can use it in Model space by setting/
increasing the text size.

TIP MTEXT

MTEXT is the keyboard command used
for text.

TWEAKING MODEL SPACE

The most common problem when creating dimensions, text and dotted lines in Model space is scale, because the annotation objects are formatted for use in Paperspace. You can easily adjust the scale of an object by selecting it and using the Properties palette.

A double click on an object will open up the properties of that object. Alternatively, use the PROP keyboard entry.

PAPERSPACE

Dimensions: While dimension characteristics will not be visible in Model space they will be in Paperspace.
Text: Text entered in Paperspace is relative to the paper size: e.g. 10pt, 14pt (equal to 10mm or 14mm), and so on in Model space.
Dotted lines: although a line will not look dotted in Model space, it will appear dotted and scaled in Paperspace.

TEXT

As we are in Model space, the units of the text in this example are equal to the drawing size: 1mm = 1 drawing unit. The text size is approximately 200mm in Model space. It is better practice to enter the size of the text in the MText dialogue.

DOTTED LINE

In Model space, you will notice from the properties of the dotted line that the Linetype scale has been increased from 1 to 200. Initially the dotted line will not look dotted in the viewpoint, so I have altered its scale in the Properties dialogue .

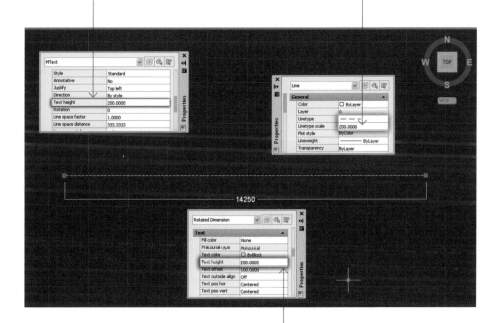

DIMENSIONS

In theory dimensioning is a simple practice. The text of the dimension measurement follows that of MText.

I have increased the text height to 200 to make the measurement visible. I have also set the offset distance of the vertical line so it does not touch the dotted line.

LOADING LINETYPES

① Select Other in the drop-down Line Properties palette

② Choose the Load option

③ Select the linetype you require

DIMENSIONS PROPERTIES

The Properties tab for the dimension line can seem endless with its many options, but by using this and a little experimentation you can set dimensions to your chosen format.

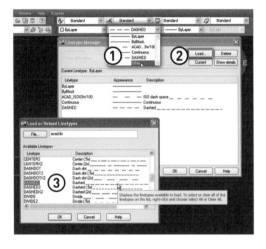

MODEL SPACE CONFIGURATION

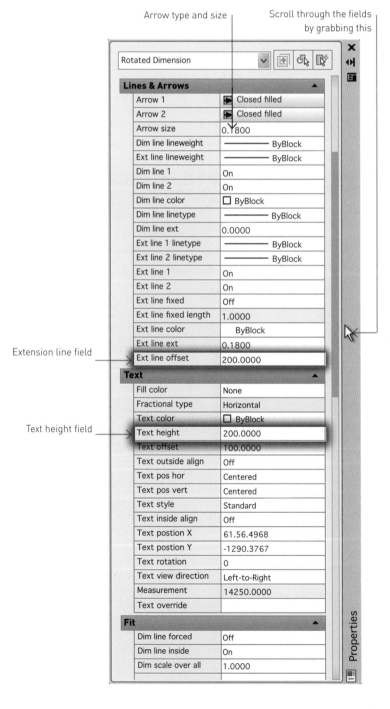

Arrow type and size

Scroll through the fields by grabbing this

Extension line field

Text height field

TIP DOTTED LINES

A simple DASHED line will be suitable for most annotation tasks. This is the most reliable in terms of scaling.

The lineweight should be one of the lowest, so as not to detract from the drawing – 0.18 or lower.

MATCH PROPERTIES

It would be frustrating to have to alter the dialogue of every line or text object individually. AutoCAD has a very powerful tool that lets you assign an existing property to another object. The Match Properties tool allows you to assign formatted lineweights, text sizes, dimensions, hatch styles and dotted lines to another object of that type. You can change a default line to a different lineweight or dotted line with a click of your mouse.

(1) Select the Matchprop tool/Keyboard: MATCHPROP

(2) Select the object and copy its properties

(3) Click on the objects you wish to transfer the properties

TIP LINEWEIGHTS

You can create a key of lineweights, dotted lines, etc. Use the Properties dialogue to format them, then use Match Properties to assign them to individual or multiple lines.

You can also use layers to organize lineweights and dotted lines, etc.

 Matchprop icon

(1) The Matchprop icon can be found here, or type MATCHPROP to activate the tool

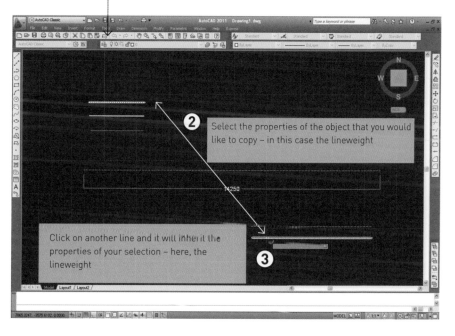

Select the properties of the object that you would like to copy – in this case the lineweight

Click on another line and it will inherit the properties of your selection – here, the lineweight

SketchUp

SKETCHUP TO LAYOUT

SketchUp Pro is supplied with an additional program called LayOut. This program is the most suitable for annotating 2D and 3D drawings. SketchUp itself has dimensions and text facilities within the program, but it does not have a lineweight or dashed line facility. SketchUp as an orthographic 2D and 3D program is excellent, but not really suitable for creating complex annotations.

If you are familiar with the paper and model spaces in AutoCAD you should find the LayOut program very similar. There are the same options to set out a drawing, carry on working in the Model space and update the drawings in LayOut. The main difference is the way that Google have bundled them as separate programs.

On the downside, the LayOut program is only available with the Pro version of SketchUp, so you will have to buy it rather than use the free version. Student licences are available and cost in the region of £30 ($50) for one year's usage. To add to the dilemma, a drawing in the free version of SketchUp cannot be saved as a useful format for importing into other programs such as AutoCAD. Again, you need the Pro functionality to be able to do this. The option to save a 2D orthographic drawing is quite an important one. You may well feel that another program may be more suitable for annotating a drawing. A drawing that you create in SketchUp may be better annotated in AutoCAD or Vectorworks, or vice versa.

PREPARATION IN SKETCHUP

You will need to alter the visual style of your SketchUp drawing before you import a view into LayOut, as LayOut imports the visual style you have in SketchUp.

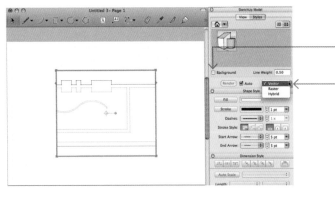

CHANGING THE BACKGROUND COLOUR (STYLES)

Deselect the Background

Set the render style to Vector

The default modelling background comes with the viewport and the drawing will plot with that shade. To set the view to white you need to deselect Background Colour and set the render style to Vector (linework).

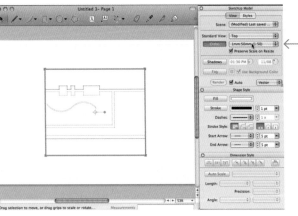

SETTING THE SCALE (VIEW)

Set your scale and view

Select the Model viewport and activate the Ortho button. You now can set the drawing to a suitable fixed scale. (Note that the scale must be relative to the drawing and paper size.) The view – top, back, front, isometric, etc. – can also be set in this dialogue.

Once you have set the scale you can alter the size of the viewport. Ensure that the Preserve Scale on Resize option has been checked.

SAVE THE SKETCHUP MODEL

When you have finished drawing in SketchUp you need to save the file, open the layout program and import the Model view (viewport) into the page setup.

PICK YOUR PAGE SIZE

When you start up Layout you will see a dialogue that will ask you to pick a paper size. This example uses A3.

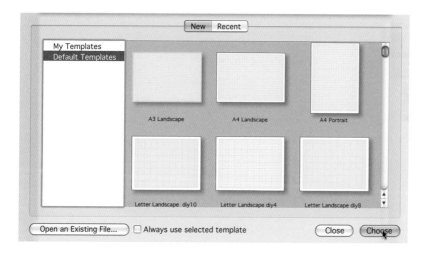

IMPORT YOUR VIEW

File › Insert. You will notice that a viewport has been created, typically with a Sketch Shade. If you follow the SketchUp-style format it will import as a wireframe with white background.

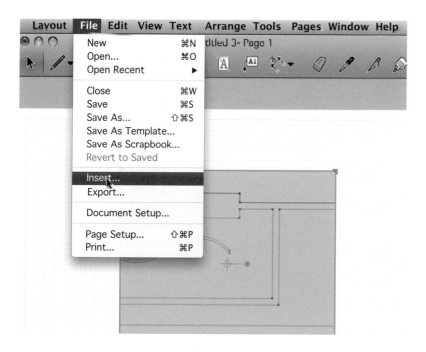

TIP REVISIONS

You can update the view in your LayOut page of a revised model by right-clicking the Model window and selecting Update Reference.

LINEWEIGHTS AND DIMENSIONS

Annotating a 2D drawing in SketchUp is a post-SketchUp process. The drawing that you have imported is still a model and is updated in the view. You can now use the LayOut program to add annotation.

When you are developing lineweights for a drawing you trace over the existing drawing, in a way not dissimilar to the way you would trace over a hand-drawn orthographic drawing.

Dimensions are very effective and easy to use; they scale themselves automatically to your chosen zoom point. You may develop your own style of dimension through the Dimension Style dialogue.

LINEWEIGHTS

① Deselect the window (viewport)

② Trace over the plan with the Line tool

③ Select the line with the Select tool

④ Change the lineweight by changing the pt thickness

DIMENSIONS

① Use the Dimension tool to specify the desired dimension

② Use the Shape Style dialogue to format the style of dimension, e.g. arrow type

③ Use the Dimension Style dialogue to change the default value from metres to millimetres

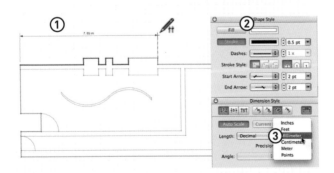

TEXT AND DOTTED LINES

The text size is relative to the paper size you have set up. Working with text is a fairly simple process, similar to the way you would use text in Photoshop. You have two ways to access the options but they differ sightly. The drop-down menu offers the option of increasing or reducing the size of the text incrementally. The Window › Show Fonts dialogue is set out in a typical text layout window.

Text tool

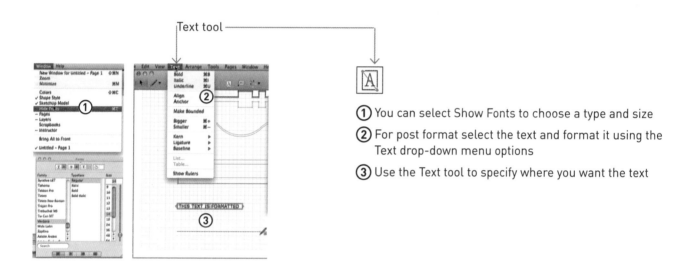

(1) You can select Show Fonts to choose a type and size

(2) For post format select the text and format it using the Text drop-down menu options

(3) Use the Text tool to specify where you want the text

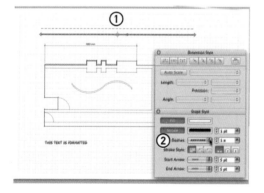

DOTTED LINES

Dotted lines are created by modifying a line style. You may also set the stroke (weight) of the dotted line and add arrows or endcaps.

(1) Draw a line with the Line tool

(2) Select the line with the Select tool and use the Shape Style menu to select Dashes

NOTE: You may also set the line to Dashes to start with, then draw a dotted line.

Vectorworks

VECTORWORKS PAGE LAYOUT

In Vectorworks you need to choose the page size before you start to annotate, as the annotation will be in proportion to the scale you set. You will have noticed while drawing the shop diagram that it is too big to fit the current American Letter format. You can either change the page size or alter the scale of the drawing.

We will now change the paper size to A3 and also change the scale of the drawing to 1:100.

① Select Document Setup by going into File › Document Settings › Document Setup.

② Change the layer scale from 1:50 to 1:100 for the drawing of the shop.

③ Change the page setup to A3, deselect the Show Watermarks and Show Page Breaks options. This removes unwanted page tiling and watermarks.

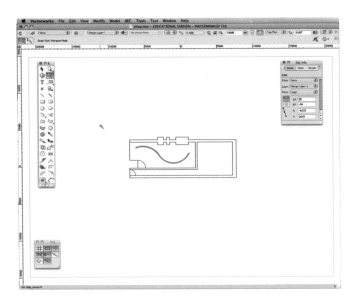

A Vectorworks A3 page layout at 1:100

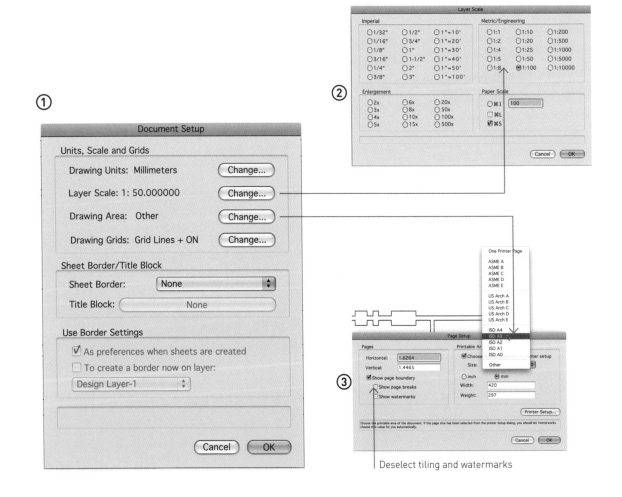

Deselect tiling and watermarks

LINEWEIGHTS AND DOTTED LINES

Lineweights and dotted lines are linked by the Attributes palette. You can define both the lineweight and the thickness of the line with this. There are various types of dotted line to choose from and they scale well if you have set the page scale. Other format options are available too, such as arrowheads and line colour.

(1) Open the Attributes palette: Window › Palettes › Attributes

(2) Select a line to apply a lineweight; deselect when complete

(3) Select another line to define as a dotted line; deselect when complete

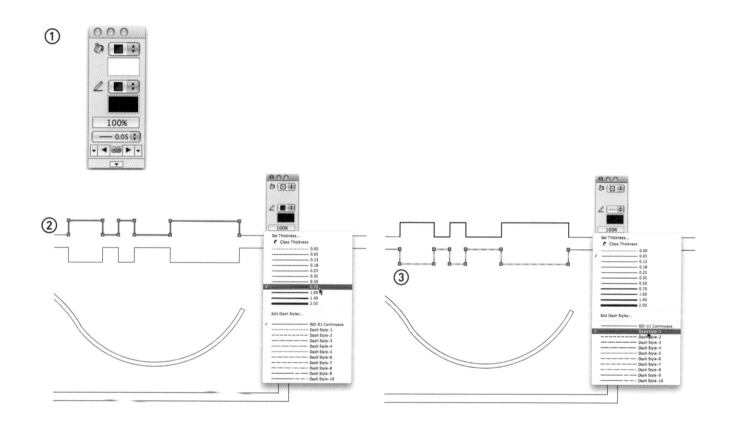

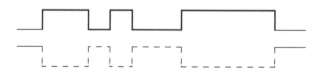

As with SketchUp and AutoCAD, you can alternatively set the attributes of the line as you draw rather than using a post-process approach.

TEXT

The Text tool is in the basic tool set. The text created is set up to be used in scaled space, e.g. 1:100. The default text size is 10, but you may format the text font, size, etc. from the Text menu.

① Activate the Text tool and click where you want the text

② If you need to format the text then select it and use the Text drop-down menu

EYEDROPPER TOOL (MATCH PROPERTIES)

Use the Eyedropper tool to post-format attributes.

① Activate the Eyedropper tool to select the object properties to copy

② Use the Alt (mac)/Ctrl (pc) key to perform the Attribute Copy command.

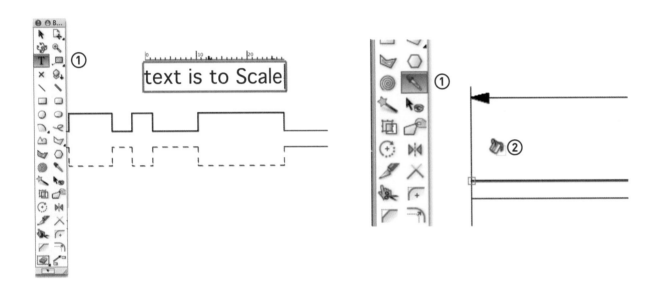

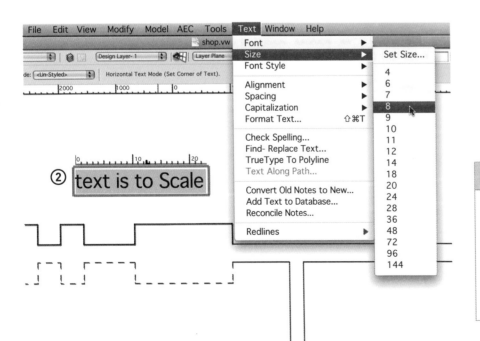

> **TIP** EYEDROPPER TOOL
>
> Once you have defined a specific style of line, dimension or text, you can use the Eyedropper tool to copy that style to other objects. This works just like the Match Properties tool in AutoCAD.

DIMENSION

The Dimension dialogue has been saved until last since it is its own entity in Vectorworks and is not related to the Attributes.

The Dimension tool resides within the Tool sets palette, which you can open via the Palettes menu. There are also some idiosyncrasies related specifically to the Vectorworks interface based on Classes, which are a type of layering system. To keep the use of dimensions simple we will set up some Class View settings before we use the Dimension tool.

Once these are set, the use of the Dimension tool is very straightforward; the scale of dimensions is relative to the page setup and you will be able to format text, dimensions, styles, etc. easily.

① Go to View > Class Options > Show/Snap Others. This ensures you can see the dimension after it has been drawn.

② Open the Tool Sets palette (Window > Palettes > Tool Sets)

③ Select the Dims/Notes field – at the top of the tool stack is the Linear Dimension tool

④ Specify a start and finish for the dimension along with the offset distance – your dimension should now be complete

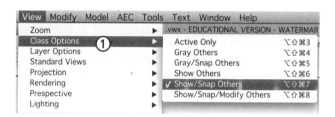

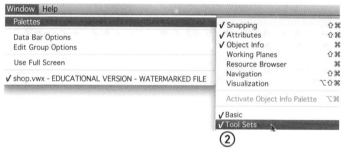

Select Dims/Notes

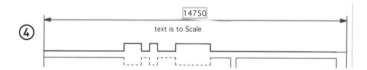

Clockwise from top left: icons for Adobe pdf; generic email; internet (Firefox); Adobe Photoshop; Adobe Illustrator; generic printer

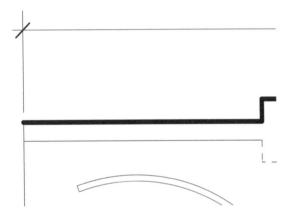

PDF
An export of the plan as a PDF. As you zoom in you will notice the line quality is good as it is a vector-based format.

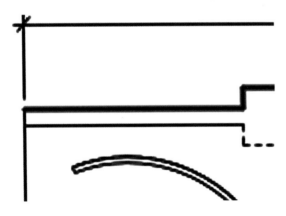

JPEG
An export of the plan as an Image file/jpeg. As you zoom in you will notice the line quality is very poor and pixillated because it is a raster-based format. You can improve the quality by upping the resolution, but this leads to very large file sizes.

PDF PLOTTING

The Adobe PDF plot is the most versatile format for the export of CAD drawings. In terms of its file structure when exported from CAD it is a vector-based format, which in simple terms means that you preserve the line quality. If you save or export the same drawing as a jpeg or a bitmap then these will be subject to pixilation. This is quite a common fault in raster-based exports.

AutoCAD, Vectorworks (the name gives the clue) and SketchUp are vector-based drawing programs. You can use these programs to plot/print out drawings directly to a printer and the results will be good.

A PDF, on the other hand, can be readily emailed, used in a web page, imported into page layout programs like Photoshop and Illustrator, and printed.

If your drawing is set up to be on an A3 sheet, for example, and has had the scale set at 1:50 then if you import that drawing as an A3 sheet and retain its proportions/resolution then it will always be to scale when you work further on it.

Overall, the most beneficial part of printing to PDF is the avoidance of waste and cost. Often when directly plotting to a printer/plotter mistakes are made, particularly the incorrect layout of drawings and lineweights. By exporting first you can check the drawing – re-export updated PDFs until you think the drawing is 99 per cent ready to print.

It is always useful to print a proof and check it through, but if you have the flexibility of a PDF you can output the print at a smaller size, and at home on your home printer rather than on a plotter.

AutoCAD plot

We will be using Model space and Paperspace to plot the annotated drawings and exporting the plot as a PDF, which is a Photoshop-friendly format.

The key command Alt + P (Mac) or Ctrl + P (pc) will activate the Plot dialogue, or it can be found by selecting File › Plot. The word 'plot' is the AutoCAD equivalent for the print function in other software packages.

The main difference between plotting in Paperspace and Model space is to do with scale. In Paperspace the scale has already been formatted by you, so the plot scale will be 1:1. In Model space it is important to set the scale to fit your chosen paper, e.g. 1:50.

MODEL SPACE PLOT

When plotting from Model space, follow these steps:

① Select the printer/plotter name – DWG to PDF

② Select the paper size. In this example I have chosen A2.
When plotting Model space it is best to select a bigger
paper size (in Paperspace you will have set the paper
size).

③ Select Window from the drop-down menu
and use the Window tab to define/select the desired
drawings.

④ Tick the Centre the plot box. It is useful to ensure the
plot fits the paper size.

⑤ Select a suitable scale for your paper size.
An appropriate scale for Model space may be
1:100/1:50/1:20.

⑥ Use the Preview button to check the plot. You may need
to alter the settings; settings to tweak are normally
Window pick or Scale.

It takes a bit of practice to get the desired results.
If you are happy with the chosen scale and the plan layout
you can right-click + Plot, or you can press Escape to
confirm the plot with OK. You will then be given the option
to save the PDF to a specific place, such as the desktop.

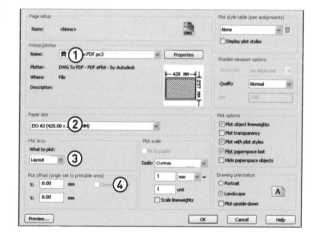

You can choose
Landscape or
Portrait in this
extended dialogue

LAYOUT/PAPERSPACE PLOT

When plotting from Layout/Paperspace the plot format will
be already formatted with scale, plotter, layout, etc. so you
just press OK and plot.

① Plotter set to DWG to PDF.

② Paper set to A3.

③ Layout already selected.

④ Centre the plot is not required.

SketchUp Layout PDF

We will now export the drawing from layout.
We have already set the page extents to A3 so we can just
export the drawing as a PDF.

LAYOUT

① Go to File › Export

② Select the PDF format (taking note of the various
options) and save the file to a convenient location

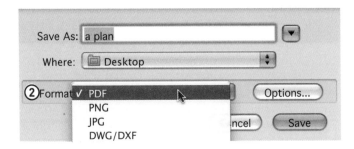

SKETCHUP PDF

You can easily save a PDF file from SketchUp Pro. If you
want to set a scale then you will need to set the scale view
first under Document Setup.

SKETCHUP

① Go to File › Document Setup

② Deselect the Fit View to Page option and set the scale –
1:100 in this case

③ File › Export › 2D Graphic

④ Select the PDF format and save the file to a convenient
location

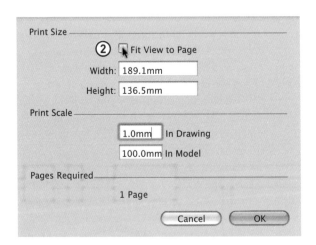

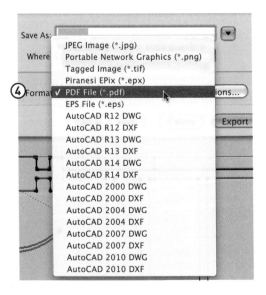

Vectorworks PDF

When you annotated the plan in Vectorworks you set up the plan scale and the page size as 1:100 on an A3 piece of paper. This will allow you to export the plot in a similar way to that completed in SketchUp layout.

① Go to File › Export › Export PDF

② An Export PDF screen will appear – at this point it might be useful to set the resolution to 300dpi

③ Save the file to a convenient location

④ A PDF screen will open after you have completed the export (note the plan at 1:100 on an A3 PDF)

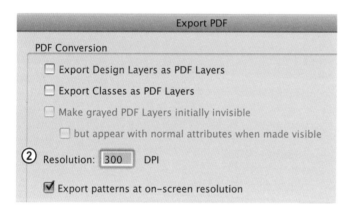

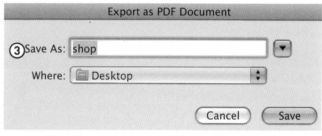

④

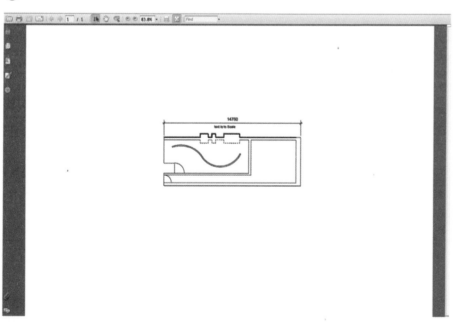

PART 2 MODELLING

Top
A simple axonometric/perspective sketch that analytically explores an object in three dimensions.

Middle
A 3D sketch model created out of scrap material. An effective and quick method of communicating a design.

Bottom
A parametric 3D computer model that has been developed to create a physical prototype using CNC fabrication techniques.

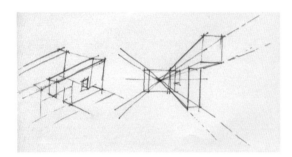

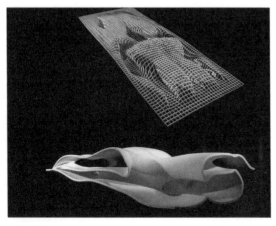

INTRODUCTION

A designer needs the ability to sketch out and explore design intentions through the development of basic volumetric forms. A sketch exploration can be developed quickly and manipulated instantly, and is essential for forming a clear concept for the development of a design to follow. In the early stages this representation can take the form of an isometric or simple one-point perspective sketch. You will often find it useful to sketch out your proposals before attempting to model a scheme in CAD.

Model making
Physical model making is also a important skill in 3D representation. From sketch to final presentation model, the medium is a very effective form of 3D communication. In many cases it can be the best way to develop and communicate a scheme. It also allows you to physically understand a scheme's 3D composition, which is then useful in forming an understanding of the way a 3D CAD model might be assembled.

Hand construction techniques
The better your understanding of hand-drawn, hand-crafted construction, the better you will be at creating 3D forms on the computer. From my own experience, drafting an isometric to scale, or constructing a physical scale model has proved invaluable in my understanding of 3D CAD construction.

CAD techniques
There are some areas of CAD 3D modelling where the territory is exclusively the realm of the computer. Parametric design tools are based on the computer's ability to create free-flowing editable forms. Mathematical formulas are performed instantaneously as the user plays with the fluid forms. These forms and shapes would be difficult or near impossible for most of us to draw by hand.

These forms can be built, then the computer model used to set up the fabrication and construction process.

The recent development in CNC and 3D printing technology also gives us the opportunity to create physical prototypes from complex computer models. We are now able to create those forms and constructions that were once impossible to create by hand, which is very exciting.

Fabrication

The ability to prototype and analyze effectively the structural integrity of such forms through CNC [Computer Numerically Controlled] routers and 3D printers engages us in a era of physical objects. The ability to actually create and manufacture the structure means that this type of parametric form and structure is increasingly being created as architecture.

Computer modelling and fabrication are to become an essential component in architectural design. The construction process of 'typical' building shells is being radically influenced with the introduction of BIM [Building Information Management, see Section 5]. BIM revolutionizes the relationship of the 3D CAD model to the physical build process.

Below
The Jellyfish House by IwamatoScott Architecture introduces us to a unprecedented era in architectural and interior modelling. The use of self-generative and parametric modelling techniques are providing us with the ability to think of form and structure in a new light. The conceptual model develops the notion of the 'smart' house, exploring rainwater collection and the use of photovoltaic's. The 3D model starts to blur the boundaries between form, surface and construction.

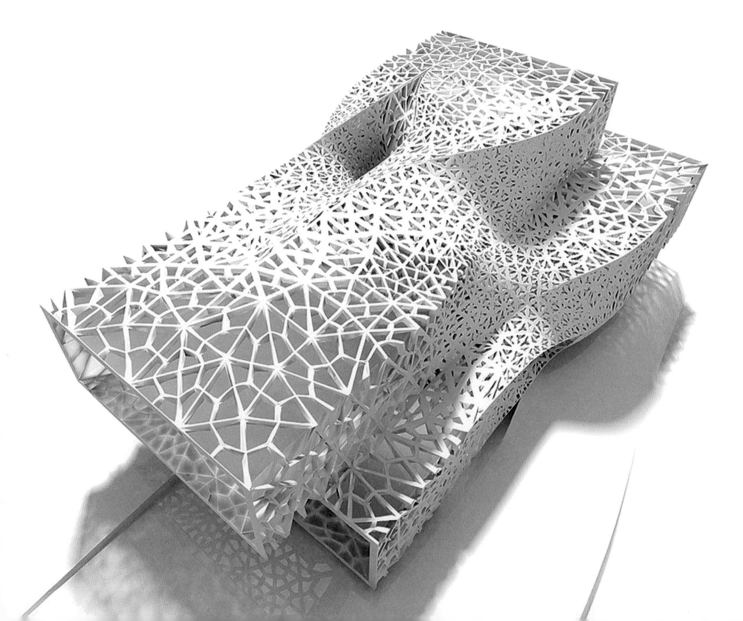

3D INTERFACES

In the 3D section you will note that there are more programs added to the collection. AutoCAD, SketchUp and Vectorworks share a similar interface to the 2D interface. With AutoCAD you may well choose the 3D modelling workspace as it collects all the tools into one toolbar, but the command line with practice is quicker. SketchUp has a larger tool set and Vectorworks an extended tool set. In all cases in 3D it is best to work with the ISO/AXO view.

3ds Max, Maya and Form Z are primarily 3D modelling programs and not generally used for 2D orthographic.

3ds Max uses a tab/pane interface to organize its object creation and modify commands, Maya uses a shelf/tab system and Form Z uses a multiple icon approach where commands can be grouped.

All the software examples are capable of completing the same tasks [apart from some limitations with SketchUp]. The interfaces are different but if you associate yourself with the different setups you should be able to use any of the programs effectively.

 **AutoCAD**

FILE IMPORT

If you have saved your file as a DWG from the tutorial in the last part then you will be able to use the File › Open command. You will find the Import command in the same menu.

INTERFACE SETUP

AutoCAD has a dedicated 3D interface that can be selected from the workspaces drop-down menu. But in keeping with a simple setup, I would recommend that the right-click tab functionality in the Classic interface is better as you can select the tools that you need for the modelling task.

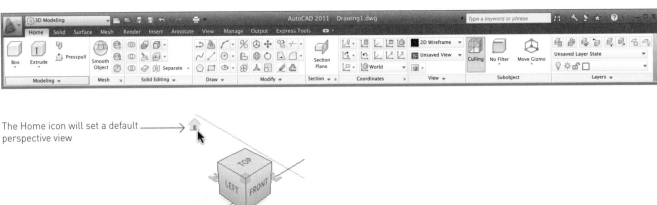

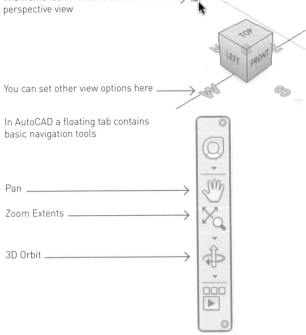

The Home icon will set a default perspective view

You can set other view options here

In AutoCAD a floating tab contains basic navigation tools

Pan

Zoom Extents

3D Orbit

TIP ZOOM/EXTENTS

In 3D space it is easy to get lost in infinity! Use Zoom/Extents to help you find your model.

AUTOCAD COMMAND LINE VS ICONS

Although the icon interface has been introduced, I would recommend that the Command Line interface is often a better way to create and modify. All the commands are listed and easily typed in, which can save you the time it takes to search for icons. Below are useful Command Line tools that you can simply type to activate.

→ BOX

→ EXTRUDE

→ PRESSPULL

→ SWEEP

→ REVOLVE

→ UNION

→ SUBTRACT

→ MESH

→ MESHSMOOTH

→ EDGESURF

→ 3DMOVE

→ 3DCOPY

→ 3DARRAY

→ 3DSCALE

→ 3DPOLY

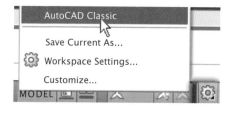

To bring up toolbar options, first select AutoCAD Classic.

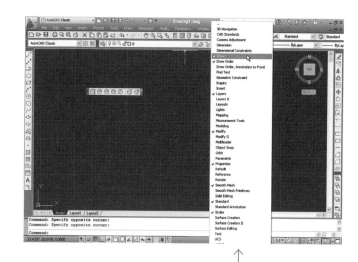

Right click for the toolbar you require.

AUTOCAD CLASSIC TOOLBARS

Selection of 3D modelling toolbars in Classic mode.

3D Navigation

Modelling

Mesh

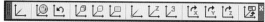

UCS

View

3DS MAX

The interface for 3ds Max is quite different to those demonstrated so far. Similar to other modelling and animation packages, it contains the entire collection of the tools you need in the interface. This is useful, but also quite intimidating for the novice user.

It would be impossible to cover the whole program here – that would be a book in itself. So just the core components that relate to basic 3D modelling will be introduced, including where to find all the tools you need. You can then refer back to this section as you work.

Direct object creation in 3ds Max is different to other programs. You have an interface with tabs. The first tab is the Create field. There is a drop-down menu that will allow you to select different object types, such as lines or helixes.

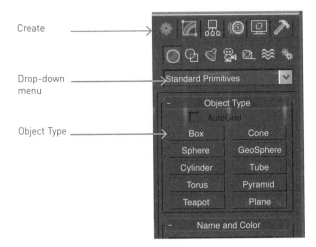

Create

Drop-down menu

Object Type

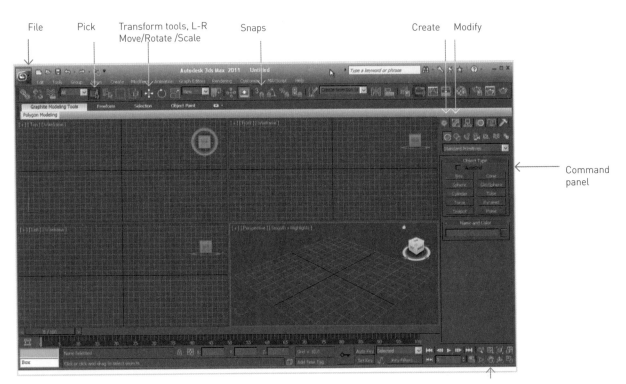

File   Pick   Transform tools, L-R Move/Rotate /Scale   Snaps   Create   Modify

Command panel

View/Camera tools

FILE IMPORT

Many file types can be imported by 3ds Max. In each case it is a simple process. You will be asked to specify what and how you want to import the file. If you import with the Entity selection you will import separate objects; without this selection it is possible that your plan or 3D model will import as a block (a whole), which can be difficult to work with later.

Import file into 3ds Max

Select file type

Import Options

Entity selection

VIEW

The ViewCube functionality associated with other Autodesk software also exists within 3ds Max. You can use this to set the viewports to top, plan and home, which is a perspective view. You can also use the scroll and pan functionality of the mouse. Holding down the Ctrl key when you do this also allows you to orbit the model.

VIEWPORT TOOLS

There is an additional set of View tools, closely related to 3ds Max's camera functionality. You can change from 4 to 1 viewport for a larger working area, and Zoom and Extents are also located here.

Zoom   Extents

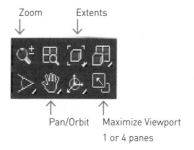

Pan/Orbit   Maximize Viewport
1 or 4 panes

TIP MOUSE NAVIGATION

- Scroll the middle mouse button to zoom in and out
- Hold down to pan
- Use the Alt or Ctrl key (dependent on software) to orbit around a 3D model

Maya

Maya is a wonderfully intuitive 3D modeller. It is associated more with animation than with architecture. In terms of compatibility with other software, especially 2D drawing programs, the software can be problematic. Maya is a very complex program, but it is also addictive!

One of the major issues you will encounter is to do with scale. Maya uses a camera setup for whatever view you choose; even if you have not inserted a camera then this is the default setting. Often when you bring 3D models into the program the imported geometry will disappear into hyperspace. You can give yourself a fair chance by scaling whatever you are working on into metres rather than millimetres. Maya likes simple units, 1–100. You can use the decimal point to be more specific and accurate.

INTERFACE SETUP

There are some similarities to 3ds Max in the interface setup, such as the position of the Move and Rotate tools. Maya employs a tab setup for creation and modification. The menu bar is also quite useful, and there is an addition sub-menu 'hot box' that can be initiated by simply pressing the space bar. It can sometimes be simpler to access this menu rather than searching for a tool or operation.

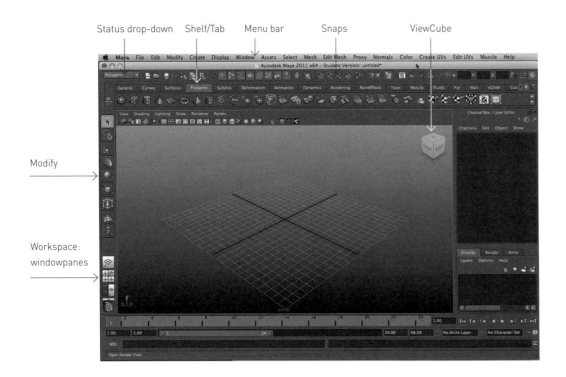

TIP ROTATING OBJECTS

Maya uses Y as the height value. So when you import a plan or object modelled in a different program it will likely be on its side. You will therefore have to rotate it into place.

TIP HOT BOX

Activated by pressing the spacebar, the hot box allows you to access nearly all the commands in Maya. You can also set the level of Object Pick and Modify from here.

FILE IMPORT

You can import many file types into Maya, including Illustrator files, but strangely the option of importing a DWG has been excluded in the Mac version of the software. You can download a free translator from Autodesk (Windows only), or if you have an earlier version of Maya (7 or 8) you could install a DWG translator plug that will do the job.

When dealing with AutoCAD DWG format, the only real option is to import in Windows, as it has DWG capabilities. Once you have created the Maya file you can then open it up on a Mac.

If you are new to Maya, you may well choose to work from scratch. Use the Lego approach to create 3D primitives and add them together. Don't forget the primary rule of scale is turned on its head as you will have to work in smaller units (1–100), which in real terms probably means working in metres.

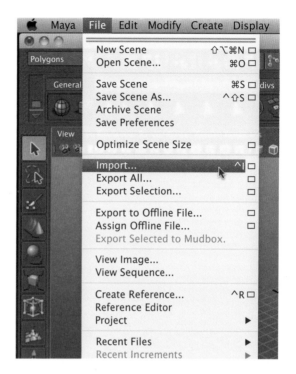

VIEW

Maya uses a default camera setup to navigate the model.

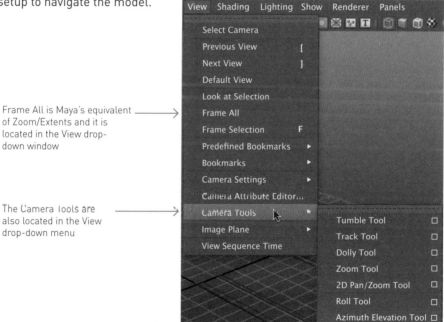

Frame All is Maya's equivalent of Zoom/Extents and it is located in the View drop-down window

The Camera Tools are also located in the View drop-down menu

Maya has the ViewCube functionality associated with other Autodesk software. You can use this to set the viewports to top, plan and home, which is a perspective view.

Form Z

Form Z is like no other software out there for 3D modelling. All the tools are there as they are in other programs but the way it works along the interface is very different.

As a modelling program it has some wonderful intuitive capabilities, especially for the creation of complex objects, such as the flower shown below.

FILE IMPORT

You can import many file types into Form Z, including Vectorworks and SketchUp. For reliability, import drawings as a DWG format.

As with most import actions, you will usually be presented with a series of options. In this DWG dialogue I have set the working units to millimetres.

Polygon tool

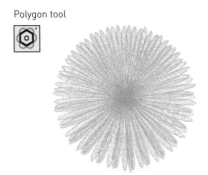

THE DEFAULT SETUP FOR FORM Z

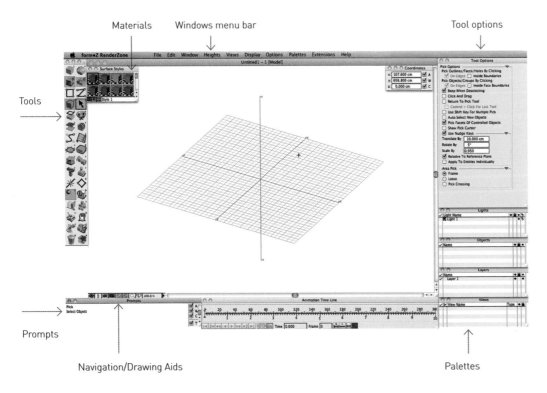

INTERFACE SETUP

It is important to set the program up correctly; the default settings are not necessarily the best settings for intuitive modelling.

In this example we have the model window as a default perspective view. I have changed the heights to Graphic/Keyed so a height can be entered manually. I have also deselected A and W in the Coordinates palette, which allows you to draw relative anywhere in the working space.

TIP IMPORTING ISSUES

If you have trouble importing a file try resaving the original file to an earlier version, e.g. 2011 to 2004 format.

TIP PERPENDICULAR

This is easy to activate by accident, allowing only perpendicular movement to be made. Deselect for freedom!

Heights set to Graphic/Keyed   Set Working Units

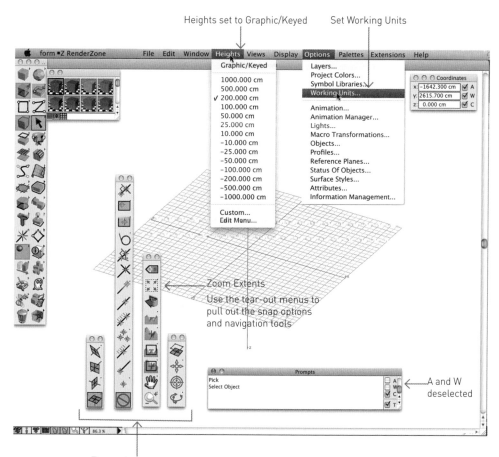

Zoom Extents

Use the tear-out menus to pull out the snap options and navigation tools

A and W deselected

Tear-out menus
(Reference planes, Snaps, Navigation)

SketchUp

FILE IMPORT

The SketchUp import functionality (File › Import) is simple, but only available in the Pro version. You have the option of importing 3ds files, which is the 3ds Max format for models or you can use the DWG option.

In 2D terms the DWG is the best option. You do have the ability to import image data, such as jpeg and PDF, but these will not allow you to snap accurately to a line as an object in space.

TIP MOUSE NAVIGATION

- Scroll the middle mouse button to zoom in and out
- Hold the middle mouse button down to pan
- Use the Alt or Ctrl key (dependent on software) to orbit around a 3D model

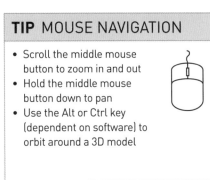

3DS and DWG formats

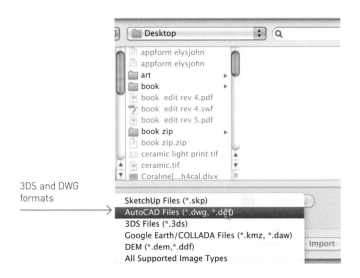

INTERFACE SETUP

In Part 1 you will have experienced the intuitive SketchUp interface. All the Zoom tools etc. work with 3D modelling. The screengrab below helps you to locate modelling tools.

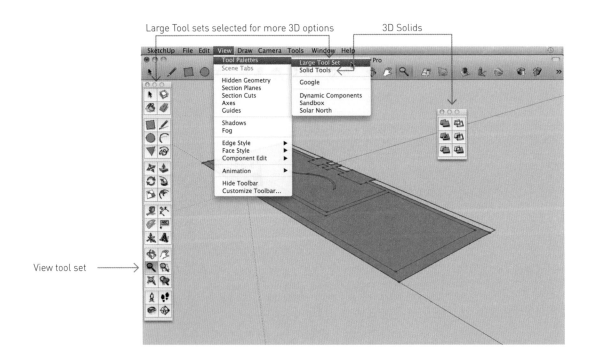

Large Tool sets selected for more 3D options

3D Solids

View tool set

Vectorworks

The 3D environment in Vectorworks is very different from other software – it is driven by its drawing interface. The 3D modelling tool set will allow you to draw primitives in plan view and isometric view. If you want to draw a 2D object then it will remain in plan view until it is converted to a 3D object.

You may find it useful to open up the extended tool sets options. Here you will find many options for the automatic creation of 3D objects.

The favoured approach to object creation is to draw 2D surfaces and then extrude them. As a method you will be required extrude 2D polygon forms before they will be shown in 3D space.

As you experienced in the 2D environment, you may well need to set the document's working units and scale in the setup dialogue; Vectorworks likes to be in scale.

FILE IMPORT

Start a new file. Pick the Architectural metric template. Once the new file is created you will be able to import your drawing. There are lots of import options, including DWG, 3ds Max), and the ability to import a SketchUp model. On import select the mm option and set the Model space to an appropriate scale.

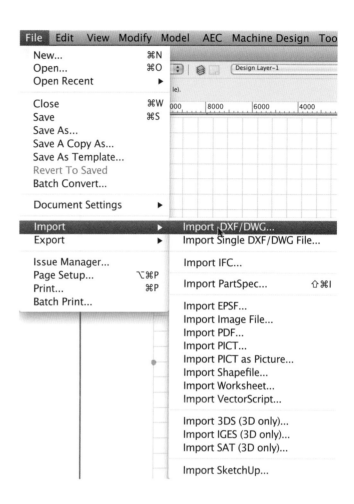

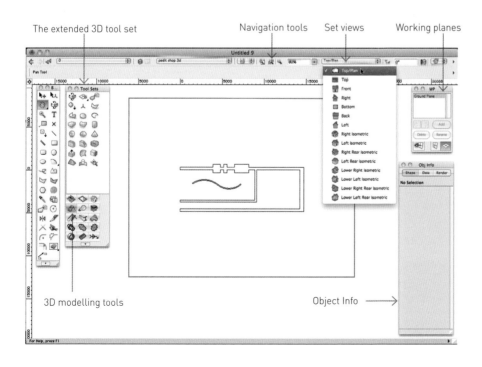

The extended 3D tool set   Navigation tools   Set views   Working planes

3D modelling tools

Object Info

XYZ

XYZ is the Cartesian coordinate system used by all CAD software. Without going into the specific science and mathematics of the system, you can think of the X and Y as the typical environment you first experience when drawing a plan; 3D modelling takes this one step further with the inclusion of the Z axis. By adding the Z axis, a 2D object is given height.

Principally, most CAD interfaces are set up with the coordinates of the working plane set to XY. Many programs will greet you with a four-plane interface. This typically has the top, front, back and perspective view, which are all the view elements needed to effectively model in three dimensions.

You can use the front/back view to draw objects or draw lines vertically; you can also extrude a face or object in that direction. By default you can return to a classic perspective view to carry on working on the ground plane and the Cartesian coordinates remain at XYZ.

Most software will allow you to rotate the XYZ coordinates to a different configuration, such as ZXY and YZX. This allows you to work in a default perspective view and to model in any direction of your choice.

It is sometimes useful to set XYZ coordinates to an angled reference if your geometry is not rectangular, i.e. at an angle of 33 degrees. You can then rotate the XYZ reference system to be in line with the geometry of your object. Different programs have different ways of doing this. AutoCAD, for example, rotates the system automatically as you use the Set View commands, front, back, etc. It can and often does leave you in a strange configuration where you can only extrude on the vertical face of an object rather than in the typical up direction of XYZ.

Programs such as SketchUp fully automate the working coordinates direction. You will be unaware that it is changing your coordinate references, which is another reason why so many people find it easy to use. The Vectorworks 3D modelling environment is built around setting the working plane, as are other programs such as Form Z, which use a method of set reference planes.

Presspull and dynamic auto tracking has in many ways replaced the need to rotate the XYZ working plane. It has an automated reference system that has the ability to pick up a face, allowing you to work at any given angle. That said, there are always times in 3D modelling when you will need to modify the XYZ system.

Direction
XYZ, the typical axis of the Cartesian coordinate system.
Red =X; Green =Y; Blue = Z

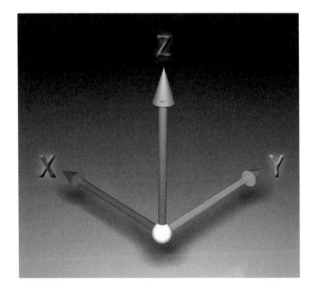

Below

The diagram shows how a typical modelling plane/
reference XYZ can rotate at 90 degree increments.
A coordinate system consists of four basic elements:

① Origin 0, 0, 0

② Axes direction XYZ

③ Choice of positive or negative direction

④ Cube created in +XYZ

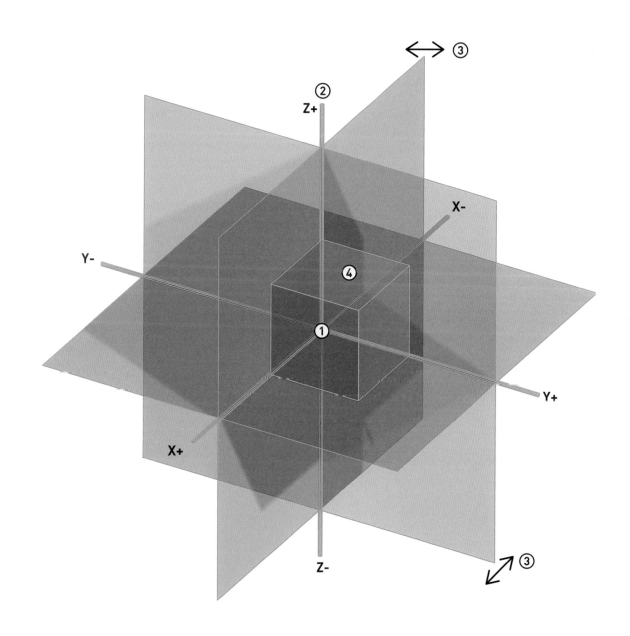

AutoCAD

DYNAMIC UCS

The simplest way to navigate around the XYZ interface is to have AutoCAD's Dynamic UCS function turned on. This will automatically pick up objects by face.

It will often unintentionally set the direction of a UCS plane to a direction you don't want.

Dynamic UCS

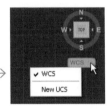

You can reset your UCS (XYZ) to → World coordinate system using the ViewCube option.

VIEWPOINT CONFIGURATION

An easy way to navigate a model is to use the Viewpoint Configuration List or select and draw in front/side views to create vertical lines.

Viewpoint Configuration List

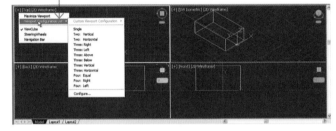

UCS toolbar

3ds Max

VIEWPORT CONFIGURATION

By default 3ds Max encourages the use of the tiled window to draw and modify objects. The perspective here shows the typical XYZ setup.

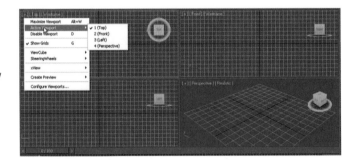

Maximize Viewport toggle

ANGLED GRID

You can use the Grid option (shown right) to create a reference grid to any angle desired. You can drawn the grid directly on an object

REFERENCE COORDINATE SYSTEM

The reference coordinate system allows you many different coordinate options in relation to creation and transformations. You can use the Pick option (View > Pick) to set the coordinates to 000 at the point of your pick, useful to create an accurate object or transform at a specific point.

Object option

Angled grid in a working window

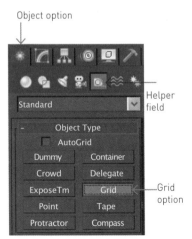

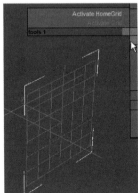

Helper field

Grid option

Maya

XYZ

Maya, unlike all the other programs, uses Y rather than Z as the height parameter. It has no option to rotate the UCS or the XYZ system. The program relies on its intuitive, organic modelling approach to allow objects to be modified in any direction.

LAYOUTS

You can use the Layouts option to draw an object in front view, plan view, etc.

Panels › Layouts › Four panes

← Viewport 1 or 4 panes

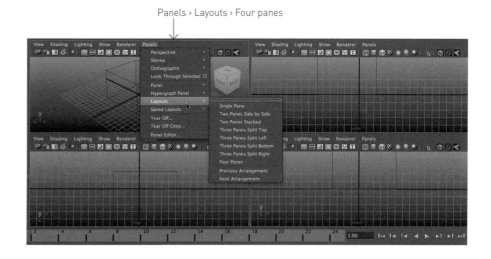

 Form Z

XYZ PLANES

You can rotate the XYZ planes in Form Z to create objects in a specific direction.

TILE WINDOWS

You can also use the Tile Windows option to create four windows (Viewports).

Reference planes ⟶

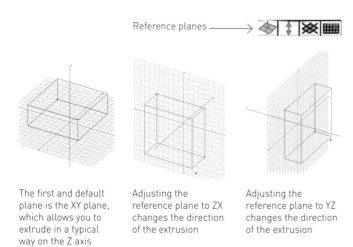

The first and default plane is the XY plane, which allows you to extrude in a typical way on the Z axis

Adjusting the reference plane to ZX changes the direction of the extrusion

Adjusting the reference plane to YZ changes the direction of the extrusion

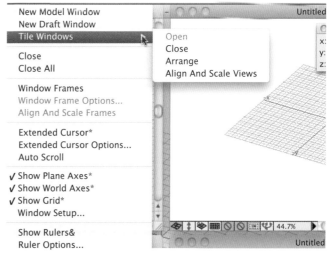

SketchUp

DYNAMIC UCS

SketchUp has a dynamic UCS built into the interface, which is why many users find it so easy to use.

XYZ ANGLES

The Axes tool in SketchUp will allow you to select a specific angle and move the XYZ plane to this direction. This is very useful for working at odd angles.

WORKING WINDOW

SketchUp has a single window to work with, there is no tile option. You can use the Camera › Standard Views menu to toggle through top, front, iso, etc.

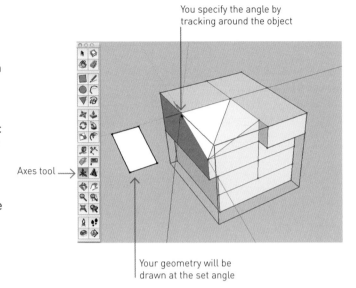

You specify the angle by tracking around the object

Axes tool →

Your geometry will be drawn at the set angle

Vectorworks

DYNAMIC UCS

Dynamic UCS tracking is a very new addition to Vectorworks and works by picking up the face/angle of objects, allowing you to draw at that angle.

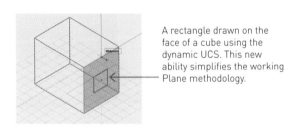

A rectangle drawn on the face of a cube using the dynamic UCS. This new ability simplifies the working Plane methodology.

WORKING PLANES

Vectorworks encourages the use of working planes in the 3D interface. This is similar to the UCS and reference planes we have seen in other software. By setting up a series of working planes you can navigate and draw in your chosen direction rather than just from the ground plane in the Z direction.

To set up a new working plane, select the Working Plane tool in the 3D Tool Sets. Once selected you will be able to select a face of an object, which will in turn set the working plane in that direction.

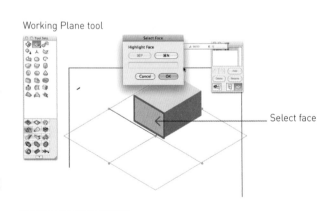

Working Plane tool

Select face

VIEWPORTS

You can use the Viewport's functionality to create multiple views on a page. This is generally done when a drawing is complete and for presentation purposes. When using the single page setup you can use the View › Standard View options to toggle through top, front, iso, etc.

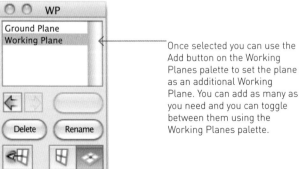

Once selected you can use the Add button on the Working Planes palette to set the plane as an additional Working Plane. You can add as many as you need and you can toggle between them using the Working Planes palette.

SIMPLE CREATION TECHNIQUES

In CAD programs there are different tools and methods that can be used to create exactly the same outcome. Taking the example of a box, you can create this directly, extrude it from a square, or presspull it with the Presspull tool. This choice is important as inevitably things will go wrong and not work! Computer modelling by its very nature is temperamental. The ability to try it a different way, such as directly creating a 3D solid rather than extruding it, is key to efficient development.

Often users will persist with the same operation, trying to make it work. The problem is often not software related but the chosen method of construction, or poorly constructed objects. While there will inevitably be the occasional late night, it is best to consider the different solutions available for one task. If at first you don't succeed then try again another way. There are nearly always at least three ways to do the same thing.

Box, Extrude and Presspull

A box/cube is a 3D solid that will in principle (depending on its segments) allow you to create any 3D form. It is a method of direct object generation, created by specifying two points and then a height.

The Extrude command allows you to derive a 3D object from a surface object. For example, a rectangle can be transformed into a box using an Extrude command; a circle can be extruded into a cylinder in the same way.

The Presspull command is an offshoot of the Extrude command. It will allow you to create a 3D solid from complex 2D surfaces by creating a field from closed objects. It will also allow you to add and subtract to a face of an existing 3D form.

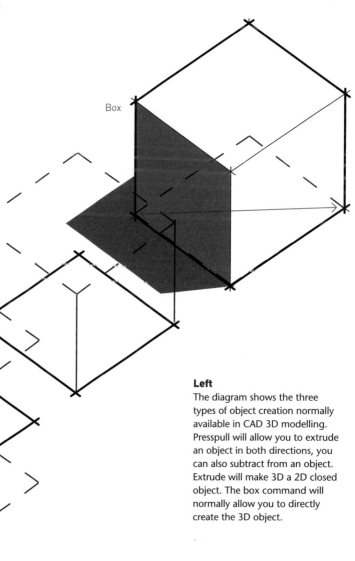

Box

Extrude

Presspull

Left
The diagram shows the three types of object creation normally available in CAD 3D modelling. Presspull will allow you to extrude an object in both directions, you can also subtract from an object. Extrude will make 3D a 2D closed object. The box command will normally allow you to directly create the 3D object.

AutoCAD

The basic Create commands are available as tool icons in the basic 3D and the Classic interface through the right-click toolbar functionality.

BOX, EXTRUDE AND PRESSPULL

The Box tool requires two points in opposite corners; you will pick these and then be asked for a height value.

The Extrude tool requires an existing object to extrude: if it is a closed object then it will be created as a solid; if it is an open object it will be a surface mesh object.

The Presspull tool needs to find a closed region/object to define its area. Beware, though – with complicated geometry it will often freeze the computer and you may lose work. As a general rule I always put a save on before using it and move the mouse over the area to be presspulled.

Command line:
BOX
EXTRUDE
PRESSPULL

Box   Extrude   Presspull

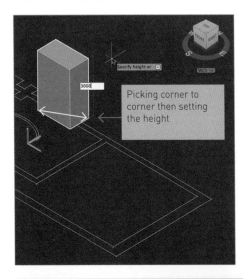

Picking corner to corner then setting the height

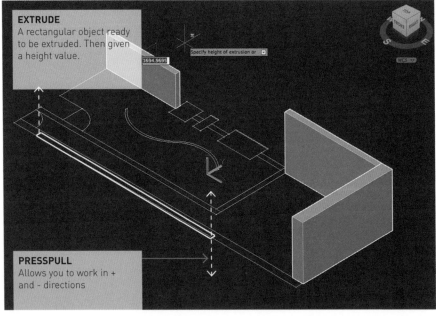

EXTRUDE
A rectangular object ready to be extruded. Then given a height value.

PRESSPULL
Allows you to work in + and - directions

TIP POLYLINE EDIT

You can join a series of lines in AutoCAD by using the PEDIT command. This will create a closed object out of multiple lines. Use your snaps for accuracy.

If you have a series of lines with gaps and they won't presspull or pedit, then trace around the linework. Use the C command as the last move and it will close the line.

3DS MAX

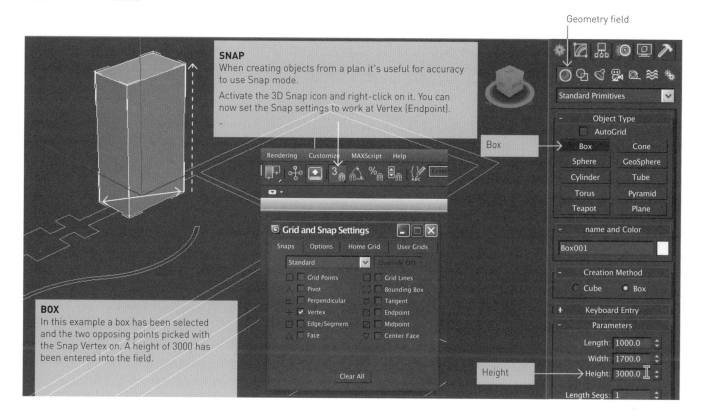

Geometry field

SNAP
When creating objects from a plan it's useful for accuracy to use Snap mode.

Activate the 3D Snap icon and right-click on it. You can now set the Snap settings to work at Vertex (Endpoint).

BOX
In this example a box has been selected and the two opposing points picked with the Snap Vertex on. A height of 3000 has been entered into the field.

Box

Height

EXTRUDE

Extrude is a tool to make your plan 3D. The Presspull operation does not exist in this interface, but if you prepare your plan carefully you can perform an equivalent operation.

Modifiers are the equivalent to many of the topology modify operations; a series of complex operations exist in this tab. In principle you can apply multiple modifier actions to any object that you create.

MODIFIER TAB

Modifiers are tools that change the shape or appearance of a created object. You can apply multiple modify actions to a single object

Some modifiers only work with certain types of object, such as meshes or splines. Multiple modifications are placed in a stack and you can go back and alter the settings at any time. The Modifier tab offers powerful parametric modelling tools.

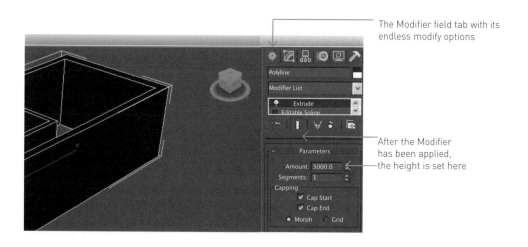

The Modifier field tab with its endless modify options

After the Modifier has been applied, the height is set here

Maya

BOX

Direct object creation in Maya is principally what the program is all about – readily editable polygon modelling. On a simple level it is as easy as drawing a rectangle corner to corner and then giving it height. In this case this is completed with the Polygon tool. You can also add subdivisions and specify the exact dimensions of the object in the Object Inputs.

Polygon drop-down

The Polygon Box tool

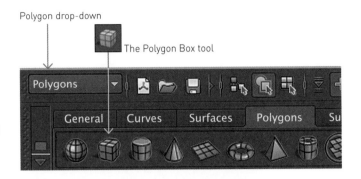

Scroll down

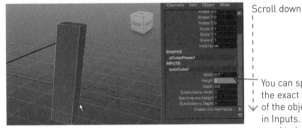

You can specify the exact size of the object in Inputs. You need to have Construction History selected to have the Inputs option

CHANNEL BOX
The Channel box editor allows you to alter an objects attributes, such as size and scale. You can also transform/ modify, such as rotating an object.

TIP CREATE IN METRES

Make sure you think in metres! Maya needs to be scaled or you will loose your extents – the model will vanish.

CREATE A POLYGON

When you bring any linework into Maya it can be very tricky to trace around objects accurately. The Create Polygon tool allows you to create polygon surfaces that can be extruded. Due to it being a polygon it is limited to rectilinear or triangular geometry.

You need to ensure you have the Polygons drop-down selected; this gives you access to the Windows menu.

A Point Snap should be selected

Trace around the plan work (with Point Snap on) and, when complete, use the Return key to close the polygon

The Create Polygon tool is in the Mesh drop-down menu. Mesh › Create Polygon Tool

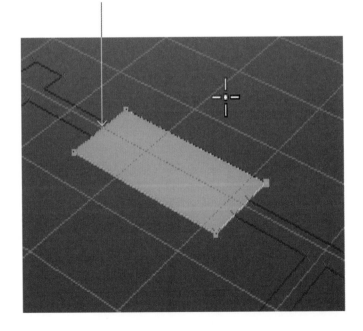

EXTRUDE

You can extrude a closed surface polygon in Maya.
The method is the same for all the types of geometry;
you just need to ensure that you are using a polygon object.
Edit Mesh › Extrude.

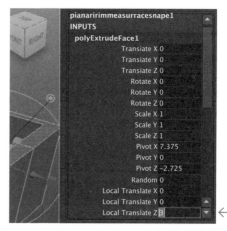

CHANNEL BOX
When selected the Gizmo will appear. Use the Local Translate field to enter the height (3, in this case) in the Z axis.

CREATE SURFACE AND PRESSPULL

Maya does not offer the Presspull function. As with other 3D software, you are advised to prepare your 2D drawing as a closed object and then you can easily extrude in a similar fashion to Presspull.

Maya is good in terms of assembling a surface from a group of lines. You can use the Surfaces › Planar command to do this. This method is suitable for creating solids out of curves and other non-rectilinear geometry. The linework is converted to a polygon surface to be extruded by the Polygon › Extrude command.

Note: You need to create a planar surface and have the surface option selected so you will be able to reference the Surfaces › Extrude command.

Select linework

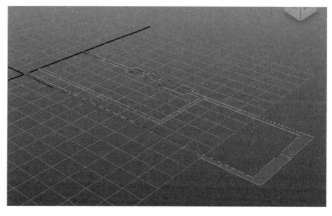

Select the surface option

Surfaces › Planar

Polygon option

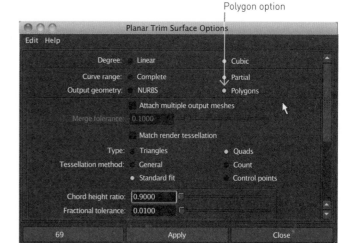

Form Z

CUBE

When using Cube Options in Form Z, select the two-point option (using a double click on the tool itself of the Tool Options dialogue). The height can also be manually specified, as I have done, by using the keyboard entry method.

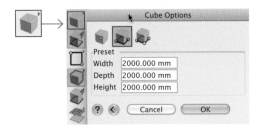

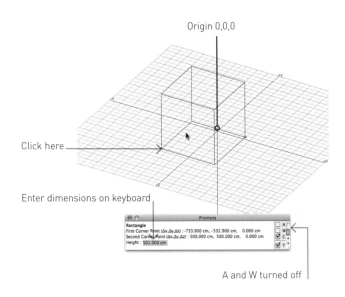

Origin 0,0,0

Click here

Enter dimensions on keyboard

A and W turned off

CREATE AND EXTRUDE

The preferred method of direct object creation is to use the Rectangle/Circle tool. This tool works in tandem with a selection of object types and is a frequently used feature in Form Z.

The Polygon/Object Type tool follows exactly the same method as the Cube tool. It gives you the flexibility to move through 2D and 3D levels, and through object types (2D surface, 2D enclosure, 3D extrusion, 3D converged, 3D enclosure.

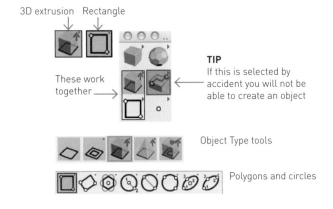

3D extrusion   Rectangle

TIP
If this is selected by accident you will not be able to create an object

These work together

Object Type tools

Polygons and circles

EXTRUDE AND PRESSPULL

Form Z does not have a dedicated Presspull command, so you will need to prepare the geometry as a closed object.

The Extrude command is located within the Derivatives tools, which is in a different location to that of the Object Creation tools.

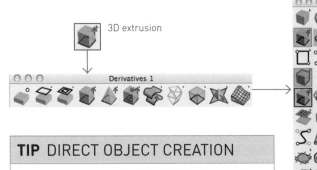

3D extrusion

Derivatives 1

TIP DIRECT OBJECT CREATION

In the working space the default A (Absolute) and W (World) space coordinate system is selected. Deselect A and W from the prompts. You can now click anywhere in the window and create an object by typing in relative sizes.

In the example of a 500mm cube you would click anywhere in the screen. In the prompts you would enter 500, 500 for the X and Y values, press enter and specify 500mm for the height [Z value].

SketchUp

BOX

There is no specific tool in SketchUp for creating a box, cylinder, etc. All objects have to be created from surfaces. You can create a solid object such as a box by grouping an object or by making it a component.

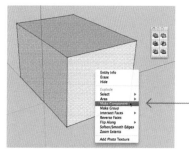

Creating a box by making a component or group

EXTRUDE AND PUSH/PULL

Object creation in SketchUp is based on drawing a 2D object and then extruding it. This extrusion in SketchUp is known more commonly as Push/Pull.

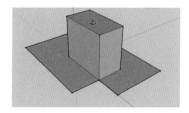

Two rectangles are drawn as surface objects and an intersection is automatically created. The geometry can then be extruded with the Push/Pull tool

Vectorworks

BOX AND 3D PRIMITIVES

When creating 3D primitives using the 3D tool set you can set the view to isometric and draw directly on the ground plane. You can draw a 3D primitive such as a box anywhere in the modelling interface.

Specify the two corners then give the object height. Select the object. You can edit the width and height using the Object Info palette.

Select the object

EXTRUDE

The interface is built to be moved between 2D and 3D environments. The simplest way to extrude a 2D object into 3D is to stay in 2D and use the Model › Extrude tool, which will allow you set a height to the 2D object. After extruding the box element you can select isometric view to see the results. If you draw with 2D tools in isometric view they will default to the plan screen until they become 3D objects.

2D plan   3D object   Iso views

PUSH/PULL

Push/Pull is a new addition to the Vectorworks interface. It works as it does with other programs – it requires a collection of lines that have no gaps, and is then able to create a field to extrude.

Push/Pull

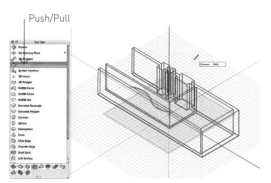

MODIFICATION

Modification is an operation that changes an object after creation. In CAD terms this can mean a simple move of an object from one area to another through to an object that transforms in shape or topology. In animation the modification process can represent the growth or transition of one object to another. The ability to modify an object allows us to create basic forms and then work on them to add increased detail or to sculpt a object.

The main transform modifications are typically Move, Rotate and Scale. They are often grouped as icons in the same field. There are many levels of these commands such as adding a multi copy to a move, which can sometimes be referred to as an array and in more complex programs multiple combined actions can be executed in one command or grouped in a stack.

You can modify an object at different levels; the first and typical level you will experience is to move an object. Further topological levels such as edge and face allow you to alter or sculpt the object's geometry. Many programs will keep a record of all the modifications you have made to an object, a history, allowing you to return to a previous state.

Meshing or adding subdivisions to a solid object such as a cube allows a greater flexibility in the sculpting of complex forms. It is often preferable to use this 'gaming' approach to create objects, as the polygon count can be suitable low in comparison to other modelling methods.

Surface object
A surface object is a collection of lines that create a closed object. The lines must intersect with no gaps. A surface object is principally a 2D plane or object, such as a circle. Surface objects: rectangle, square, circle, polygon, 2D enclosures

Simple 3D solids
Box, sphere, cylinder, cone, pipe, 3D enclosures

Object topology
You can select and modify a 2D/3D object by topological level. These elements are commonly revered to as: point or vertex, segment, face, object.

You can use the Pick, Move, Rotate and Scale tools to perform modifications on any object.

Below
The topological levels of a cube

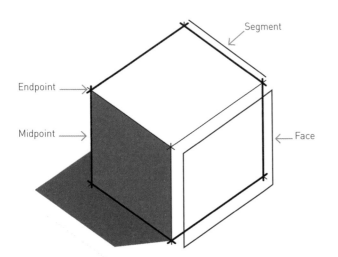

Right
A cube moved by Point [also known as Vertex] Edge [also known as Segment] and Face

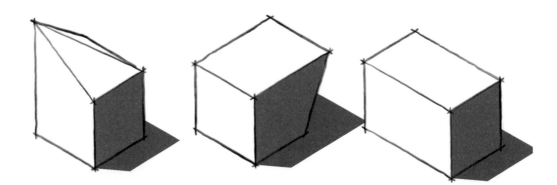

Faces and facets

Every true 3D object is made up of faces. A sphere is actually made of either triangular of rectangular faces; its smoothness is dependent on how many faces or facets it has. A box object can be initially made up of six faces, but in most modelling programs this can be increased with subdivisions.

The diagram to the right shows a box that has had three subdivisions applied to all faces. The sphere has had 12 subdivisions applied to it so you can clearly see the make-up of flat rectangular and triangular geometry. Faces or facets can be referred to as 'meshes'. In nearly all cases the object is referred to as a 'polygon object'.

Polygon modelling is a very efficient way of creating complex objects. Typically, the fewer the faces, the faster the object will render; this is quite important if you have lots of objects in a model. These low polygon objects are often used in real-time applications such as video games because they can be very efficient objects.

Subdivisions and topology

If a simple object, such as a box or a sphere, has had subdivisions applied to it, it can easily be modified and sculpted. This is how most objects start life in animation – as a singular object.

This method of construction/manipulation is equally important when creating 3D models. The terraced house shown to the right was created from a singular box that had subdivisions applied to it. The subdivisions were then manipulated to create the house. This employed a relatively small file size considering the complexity.

The third diagram shows a sphere and box that have been manipulated using the various edit options available to us. A face has been extruded, a point has been moved and a segment of the object moved. Various software programs use different terminology to describe these topological points but they are all the same in principle.

Above
An example of the subdivision of a sphere and cube, the sphere uses triangular geometry to resolve the poles.

Below
This model of a house began as a single cube: subdivisions were added to sculpt and create the final model.

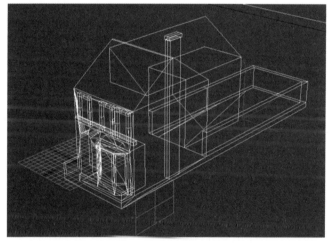

Right
The sculpting of a faceted/subdivided sphere and cube.

AutoCAD

OBJECT MODIFY

In AutoCAD you can use all the 2D Object Modify commands in 3D space; the 3D commands give you the option to work with the Z axis. Some tasks may even be performed better with the 2D tool equivalent, as this will ensure the object stays on the ground plane. When you use the 3D tools you will be able to move using the Gizmo interface.

COMMAND LINE:

3D MOVE
3D ROTATE
3D SCALE
3D ARRAY

3D Move, Rotate, Scale, Array

TIP DISTANCES

You can type a set distance into the field to perform an accurate distance to move by.

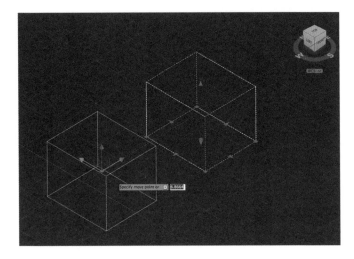

AutoCAD's 3D Move Gizmo, allowing you to move a 3D object by axis

TOPOLOGY MODIFY

There is a specific mesh section in the 3D modelling environment, but you can get these tools quite easily using the command line: MESH COMMAND.

The Mesh option will create a subdivided box or, with additional options, it will create a sphere, etc.

The Smooth Object tool will allow you to convert an object to a mesh object or increase/decrease the number of subdivisions.

Mesh Box, Sphere

TOPOLOGICAL LEVELS

Occasionally, when dealing with a complex 3D model you will want to modify the topological level. In AutoCAD it's not obviously apparent where this functionality is. You can modify by snap points – endpoint, midpoint, etc. – and you can modify by grips.

TIP EDGESURF

A little-known command in AutoCAD is EDGESURF. This keyboard command allows you to create surfaces out of connected lines. It will map a surface to any collection of lines, X, Y or Z directions, as long as they are connected

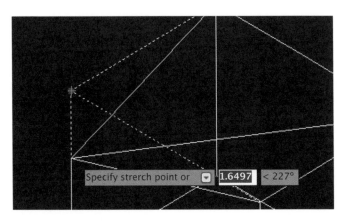

You can modify the point or edge of an object by using the CTL Pick function. This can be activated by pressing the CTL key as you pick an object.

3DS MAX

OBJECT MODIFY

3D MOVE, ROTATE, SCALE, ARRAY

The Move, Rotate and Scale commands are all conveniently located in the top menu bar. You can perform more complex operations such as Array by activating an input field from the Tools menu.

SHORTCUTS

→ W for move

→ E for rotate

→ T for scale

These are found conveniently all in a row on the keyboard.

POLYGON SUBDIVISION, MESH

Polygon subdivision is inbuilt within the 3ds Max environment. You can specify subdivisions at the point of creation or the subdivisions can be added later by selecting the object and using the Modify tab.

As with subdivision, the topological levels are integral to the interface. The easiest way to activate the Pick selection is to right click on an object and select the Edit option, which in this case is Mesh.

TOPOLOGICAL LEVELS

You can edit the topological levels of an object, such as a vertex, segment, face, etc., by right clicking on the polygon object and selecting Convert to Editable Mesh. You can also select this option in the Modifiers tab.

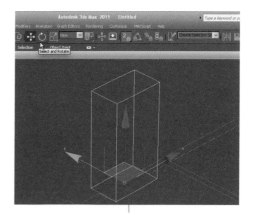

Move, Rotate, Scale

TIP LOST GIZMO

If you lose your snaps or your Gizmo then press X to reactivate them.

XYZ Move Gizmo

The Modify tab, for adding subdivisions after an object has been created.

← Segments fields

The selected level of this move is Segment. If you want to return to Object select that level. They are interchangeable as you use the Edit command.

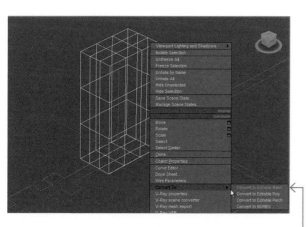

A right click pick on an object, showing the Editable Mesh option selected

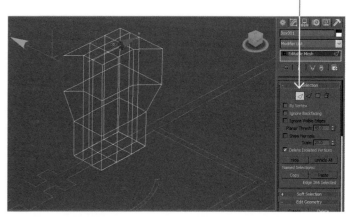

Maya

MOVE, ROTATE, SCALE

The Move, Rotate and Scale tools work with the Gizmo operation found in other Autodesk software. By default, the centre of any of the Transform tools may not be at the point or axis that you require, so you may well need to specify a point or vertices before trying a move or scale.

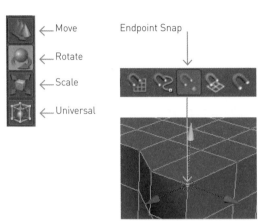

← Move
← Rotate
← Scale
← Universal

Endpoint Snap

Maya has a very useful snap-to-two-points facility – if you preselect two points they will snap together automatically

---

TIP SHORTCUTS

You can use the shortcut keys to toggle through the manipulators:
Q = pick   W = move
E = rotate   R = scale
Y = last tool used
You can use the snaps to help you pick a point to move, rotate and scale.

Channel Box

POLYGON SUBDIVISION, MESH, TOPOLOGICAL LEVELS

After the polygon box is created you can use the Channel Box/Polycube Inputs dialogue and enter the number of subdivisions.

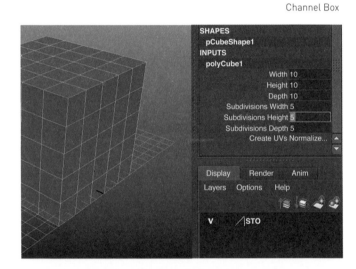

TOPOLOGY SELECT

With a right click you can select the topology of the mesh, vertex is the point of the object, face will select a segment, edge will select an edge. You can use the Shift key to add to the selection.

If no inputs are shown in the Channel Box then check that your Construction History is turned on in the status line.

You can use the Display option to show the vertices on a object. This allows for quick pick and modify actions.

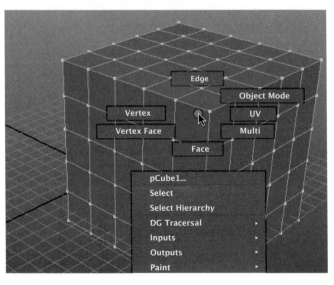

 **Form Z**

COPY, 3D MOVE, ROTATE, SCALE

In Form Z, all these commands are included in the Geometric Transformations dialogue. Similar to the Object Create tools, these work in tandem with another level, which is Self/Copy. You need to select the option on both levels. Form Z does not rely on a Gizmo to move objects but rather on snaps and placement.

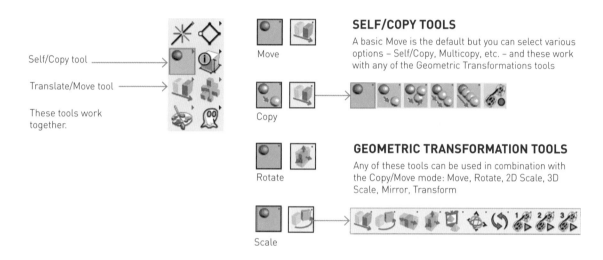

Self/Copy tool

Translate/Move tool

These tools work together.

Move

Copy

Rotate

Scale

SELF/COPY TOOLS

A basic Move is the default but you can select various options – Self/Copy, Multicopy, etc. – and these work with any of the Geometric Transformations tools

GEOMETRIC TRANSFORMATION TOOLS

Any of these tools can be used in combination with the Copy/Move mode: Move, Rotate, 2D Scale, 3D Scale, Mirror, Transform

POLYGON SUBDIVISION/MESH

You can use the Mesh tool to add subdivisions to an object. A double click or the Tool Options palette will allow you to specify the number of subdivisions.

NOTE: You need to create an object such as a box to apply the mesh operator.

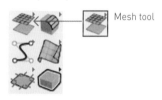

Tool Options palette

Mesh tool

TOPOLOGICAL LEVELS

Topological levels work with the Pick/Modify commands and have all the levels of point, segment and object as found in other 3D programs.

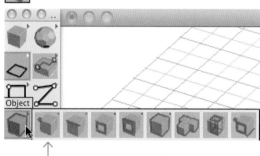

Object level

Object

Left to right, from this icon: Point, Segment, Outline, Face, Object, Group, Hole, Volume Automatic

TIP TOPOLOGICAL LEVELS

When you go to move or pick an object in Form Z, you may find that the topological level has been changed from Object to Point, only allowing you to move an object's point. Change the level back to Object and the whole object will move.

SketchUp

OBJECT MODIFY

MOVE , ROTATE, SCALE

There are no specific 3D transform tools in SketchUp; the Move, Rotate and Scale tools are the same as the 2D tools. The tools have no Gizmo.

Move, Rotate, Scale

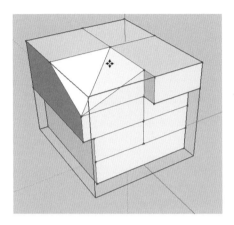

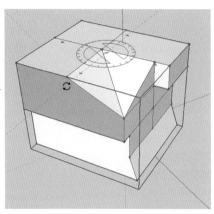

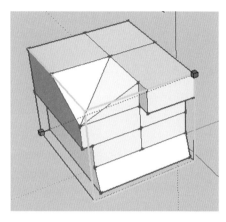

The Move tool will allow you to move in any of the XYZ directions.

NOTE: The Move tool will only move the face. You will have to select the geometry or group to move the whole.

When the Rotate tool is selected in a 3D environment you will be presented with a protractor so that you can specify the axes and the angle of the rotate.

The Scale tool is similar to those of other 3D modelling programs but has no Gizmo. You can select to scale in an axis direction or, if you pick centrally, you can scale in proportion.

SUBDIVISION/MESH

There are no subdivision or mesh tools in SketchUp. The program has plugins instead that will do the equivalent through the Ruby Console.

That's not to say that you can't construct your own meshed object using the Line tool. Using the midpoint option here I have subdivided this cube object.

TOPOLOGICAL LEVELS

The levels of point, edge and face are all present intuitively with the modelling interface. SketchUp automatically tracks to the topology.

Line tool

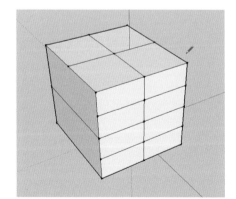

Using the Move tool to move point _____

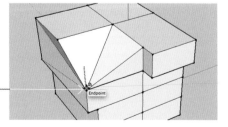

◉ **Vectorworks**

COPY, 3D MOVE, ROTATE, SCALE, ARRAY

2D MOVE

You can move an object in 2D mode with the 2D Select tool. When the object is moved a square field will appear. The object will remain on the ground plane in this mode.

3D MOVE

When the 3D Move tool is selected you can move an object easily on the Z axis.

ROTATE

The Rotate menu will allow you to rotate by 90 degrees, flip horizontal, etc.

SCALE

You can scale interactively or be more precise with numeric input.

WINDOWS MENU

You can be very accurate in Modify Operations by using the Windows > Modify command, which will let you type in an exact distance to move an object by. The interface is based on the drop-down menu rather than an icon interface.

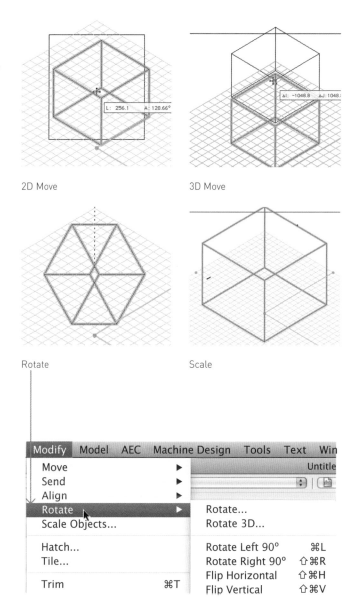

2D Move

3D Move

Rotate

Scale

MESH

You can use the Modify/Convert to Mesh command to add subdivision to an object such as a sphere. You will then be able to edit the individual vertices, edge and face. Vectorworks does not lend itself to subdivision of meshes as other programs do. Objects created with the Sweep/ Rotate tools will be meshes with subdivisions by default.

TOPOLOGY MODIFY

Topology modify is generally restricted to polygon objects rather than solids.

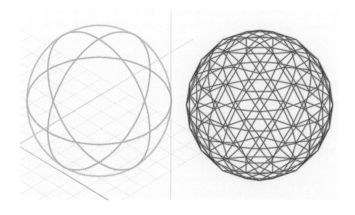

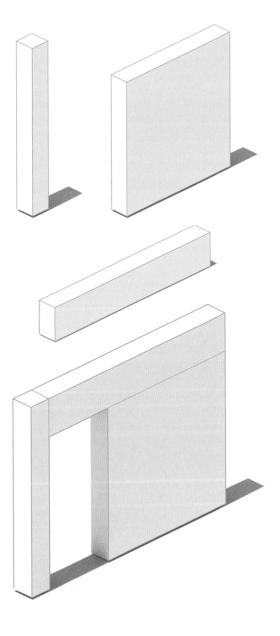

Subtract　　　Union

Sweep

Lathe/Revolve

METHODS OF CONSTRUCTION

Add and subtract booleans modifiers

Union and Subtract are the universal commands for adding or subtracting from a 3D solid.

By placing one object inside another we can subtract from a 3D object, using the Subtract command.

By using the Union command we can add to an object; this command joins the two to become one object.

Sweep and Revolve object

There are various other object generators and modifiers that are commonplace in the 3D modelling environment, such as Sweep, Revolve, Terrain, meshes, parametric and nurbs, just to mention a few!

Additive

A simple and alternative method of construction to that of 2D to 3D is what I refer to as a 'Lego' approach to construction. This would be the recommended method of creating a model in Maya. If Presspull or Extrude fails us then this can be another way around the situation.

Most children have made models out of Lego, and this building block approach to 3D CAD modelling can be easily adopted as a simplified method of construction. You can create the individual elements, then piece them together to make more complex elements such as the facade of a building with windows and door openings.

This method of construction relies on the boolean commands such as Union to transform the objects into one. The Group/Join command may also be used to group objects rather than merge them. This is a very tactile, realistic method of construction.

Left
Three primitive objects have been created in MAYA and then assembled to create a wall with a door opening. The elements are created as separate entities and then unioned together.

Subtractive

Quite often it is easy to mass up a model to get the overall form of the object, but you will often need to create openings such as doors and windows.

You can subtract an opening from an object by using another object as a element to subtract with. This relies heavily on the accurate placement of the object to be used as the subtraction. You need to ensure that it has an overall width and height that makes a clean subtraction. If the object is placed inaccurately, leaving odd angles or part of a face remaining, then it can quite often cause the file to become corrupt. This often causes a program to crash as it tries to work out bad geometry.

A way that you can ensure the accuracy of the subtraction is to make sure that it is flush or even wider than the original object that it is to be subtracted from. Another helpful method is to create a placing block that will be used to accurately drop the object into position, then delete that object after it has done its job.

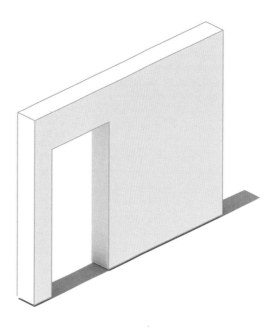

By performing a subtraction from a single box object you have a solid form that does not require the Union command

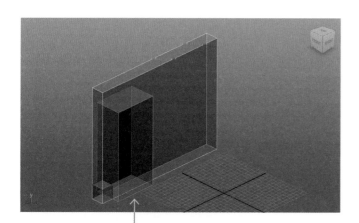

It is good practice to make the object that you are using for the subtraction bigger than the object you are subtracting from

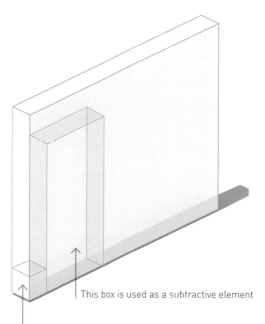

This box is used as a subtractive element

A box is used to help place the subtraction object. It is deleted after the boolean operation.

Framed construction

Sweep is a very powerful command for creating a skeletal or framed structure such as I-section steel work. You can create a line framework and then apply a section to it. It will often, if the lines are joined together, allow you to deal with awkward junctions. This tool can be especially effective when trying to create a flowing balustrade detail. If you can break down a complex object into line construction you can often speed up your modelling efficiency and create a high level of detail.

The example on the right uses a continuous 3D polyline that travels in the X, Y and Z directions. A circle is then created and swept along the line to create the 3D object. This is the circle object that gets swept along the line/path. As the line is continuous rather than broken it will resolve the corner junctions for you.

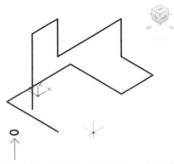

This is the circle object that gets swept along the line/path.

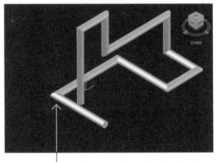

As the line is continuous rather than broken it will resolve the corner junctions for you.

Irregular planes

In 3D space the line can be a great way of creating a closed object that is at an irregular angle, such as a sloping roof or angled ceiling. You can use the Polyline/Line tool to trace and pick points that set up an angled plane. You can often use the C command to close a line or a double click.

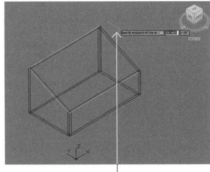

When picking the points on this angle I have left the last point open and use the C command to close the object.

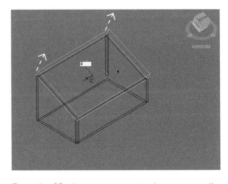

From the 2D plane you can extrude or presspull the face to make it a 3D object. The roof structure will now extrude in the direction of the angled plane.

> **TIP** 3DPOLY
>
> In AutoCAD there is a command called 3D Polyline. Use this rather than the Polyline command as it allows you to draw in the Z direction. The command line entry is 3DPOLY.

Using grids and meshes

Grids

All software has the capability to create a grid; you can alter the grid distance and the snap distance. This is very useful if you have a model that is at regular increments. Like the use of graph paper it also allows you to work with a certain amount of freedom and accuracy.

You may find it useful to create your own grid in 2D; this may not be at all representative of the final object but rather points in space that you need to create your form. You used a simple grid system in the drawing tutorial on page 24 – some of the lines were there to help you find points rather than as part of the final drawing.

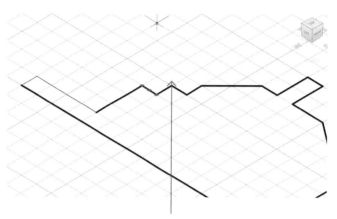

Using Grid Snap to snap a line to points on a grid. The points of snap can be angular as well as horizontal and vertical.

Meshes

Meshes or subdivisions are useful for manipulating an object. In terms of a construction grid they are also very useful. We can use or apply a mesh with subdivisions at set distances to help us draw complex subtractions from an object. We can use a planar (2D) mesh as a temporary wallpaper/graph paper. This is sometimes easier than changing the XYZ working planes.

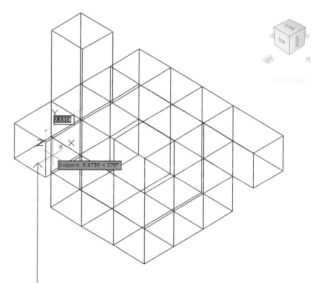

Creating a meshed object and adding boxes to the mesh object.

AutoCAD

ADD AND SUBTRACT

When performing a Union select all the items you wish to make whole and press Enter. When performing a subtract you will be asked to select an object to use for the subtraction. Press Enter when you have selected and then select the object you wish to subtract from.

Union Subtract

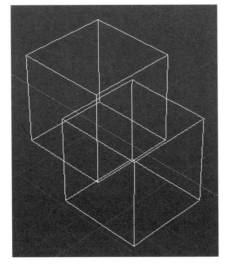

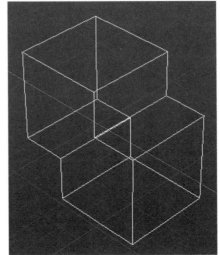

Two cubes unioned
together

SWEEP, REVOLVE

The Sweep tool requires two operands – firstly the section or object you wish to use and secondly the path or line you wish the object to follow. As is typical in the AutoCAD interface, you will have to press Enter to move on to the next selection.

Revolve requires a shape or object to revolve. If it is a closed object it will be solid; if it is an open shape it will be a surface object. After selecting the object to revolve you will be asked to specify an axis – this will dictate the direction of the revolve.

TIP CMD + Z/CTRL + Z

At all times read the command line as it lets you know what the next move is. If you make a mistake then use Cmd + Z (mac)/Ctrl + Z (pc) to go back a step and try again.

Sweep Revolve

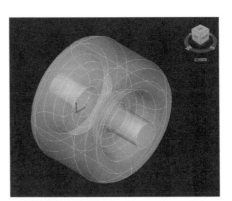

3DS MAX

BOOLEAN

Boolean moves in 3ds Max are available at many levels. The simplest form of the union and subtraction operations are those related to 3D objects.

This operation is located in the Compound Objects drop-down, which is in the same field as the Geometry field.

Geometry field   Compound Objects

The Union command

The ProBoolean option is the easiest option to work with. It allows you to perform additive actions. Select one object and then use the ProBoolean operation to add as many objects as you require to a Union or Subtract. Further operations, such as subtractions, can be found in the standard boolean operator.

SWEEP AND LATHE (REVOLVE)

The Sweep and Revolve tools also reside in the Modifier tab. Both rely on a section to generate form.

LATHE

The Lathe modifier requires one operand to create the turned object.

The Lathe modifier

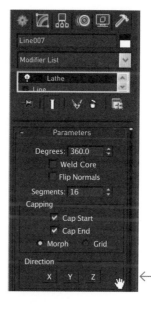

To get the correct results you need to specify the correct YXZ axis, but this can be done in real time, so eventually you will get the correct one.

There are lots of other options available to you, such as the angle of the revolve, capping, mesh, etc.

SWEEP

The Sweep tool in 3ds Max requires two operands – one being the section, the other the line or path that you wish to sweep. If you select a line or object you will be able to assign a predefined section to it or the one you have created.

The Sweep modifier

Predefined sections that can be applied to a spline.

Use the Pick option if you want to use your own selection

Maya

BOOLEAN

In Maya the boolean operations are located in the Mesh panel. Go to Mesh › Booleans. You need to have the Polygons menu selected to access the Windows menu; you may have it set to surfaces or another of the options. The Union, Difference and Intersection tools are all in this field.

There is also a Combine tool that will allow you to select multiple objects and combine/union them together.

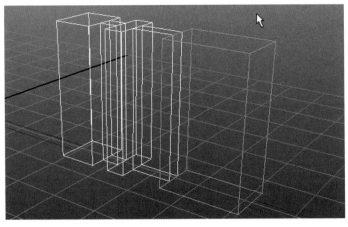

Separate objects in a position to be unioned. The objects need to be touching with no gaps. If you open the Booleans dialogue you can use it to apply multiple boolean operations.

SUBTRACT

Using Subtract select the object to be used as a subtraction first and then, using the Shift key, select the object to have the subtraction applied to.

You will note that I have made the subtraction object bigger to ensure it will be cleanly subtracted.

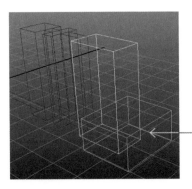

Oversized box used for subtraction

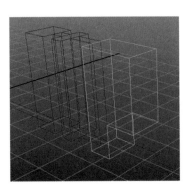

SWEEP

The Sweep operation is performed by creating an extrusion in the Surfaces dialogue. You need to select both the shape and the path. The path should be selected last. If you select the box icon next to the extrude it will bring up the Input dialogue so you can tailor the settings. In this example the setting is flat and at profile.

Path

Shape

REVOLVE

Revolve is also based in the Surfaces dialogue. You need one section/shape to rotate. By selecting the box icon you can bring up the input dialogue.

The axis of rotation is at origin 000, and as this is Maya it revolves around the Y axis.

Revolve ⟶

Form Z

BOOLEAN

Union, Subtract, Intersection

The boolean commands in Form Z are contained in the Boolean tools pull-out. You select the first object and then the next. In the case of unioning a few objects together, it is best to preselect them and union together in one operation.

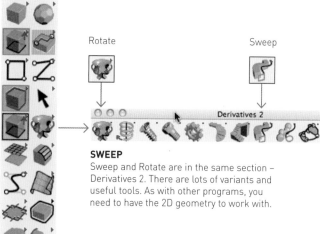

Rotate

Sweep

Booleans and intersections

SWEEP

Sweep and Rotate are in the same section – Derivatives 2. There are lots of variants and useful tools. As with other programs, you need to have the 2D geometry to work with.

SWEEP

As in most cases, Sweep needs a section or shape to sweep along a path. As Form Z provides you with a Prompts palette, similar to AutoCAD's command line, it is best to read it as you create the object.

In the Preview pane it's possible to specify the density of the sweep – the number of times the object is used along the path. You can also alter scale and rotation.

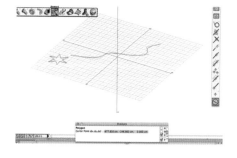

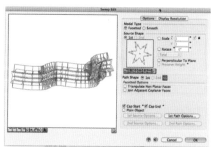

ROTATE

Form Z Rotate (Lathe) is a little different to the tools in other programs. You need to have a line as an axis. Two operands are needed. Note that the shape and the axis (path) must not intersect.

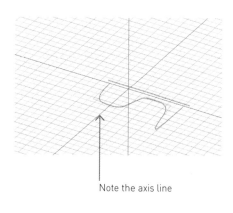

Note the axis line

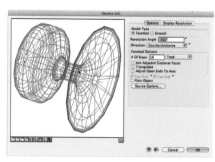

SketchUp

BOOLEAN

You cannot perform a boolean move on a surface object, and most of the geometry you create in SketchUp is made up of surface objects.

You can use Push/Pull to create openings. Delete will also remove any field that you have drawn so you will typically use these commands for boolean moves.

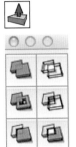

SketchUp provides boolean tools with the Solid Editing tool box. You can only perform a true boolean move on a 3D solid. To turn an object into a 3D solid you need to select the geometry (right click) and either group it or make it a component.

TIP CREATE SPHERE

You can use the Follow Me tool to create a sphere.

SWEEP

Similar to other 3D software you will need a shape/section to extrude along a path. Select the shape first and the use the Follow Me tool to extrude along the path. The form created has no options to tweak.

 Follow Me tool

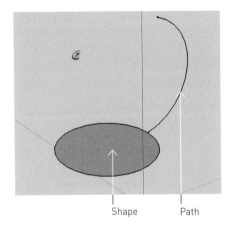

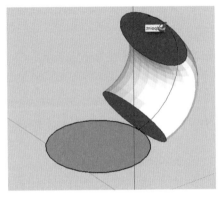

Shape　　　Path

REVOLVE

The Follow Me tool needs a field or closed shape to revolve. You need to draw a circle to track around – this acts as the path the revolve follows; it should be bigger than the surface you are trying to revolve.

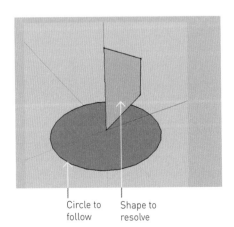

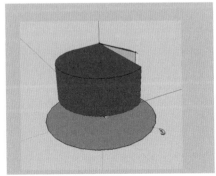

Circle to follow　　Shape to resolve

Vectorworks

BOOLEAN

The boolean tool set is contained in the Windows/Model tab. The term 'union' is not used. You can add solids, subtract solids, and quickly derive a section of a model. For architectural purposes, the Section tool is very useful.

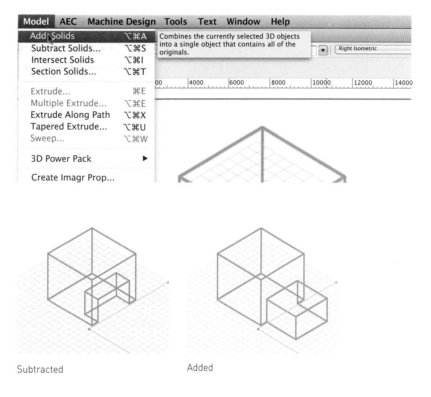

Subtracted   Added

REVOLVE

The Revolve tool is based on the Sweep tool, which may seem confusing. You need to prepare a section to revolve (sweep). You also need to specify the point at which the object will be revolved. Vectorworks uses the Locus Point tool to do this.

Note: This section was drawn, and the Locus Point added, in front view.

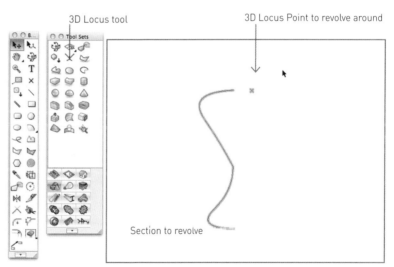

SWEEP

Sweep uses the Extrude option. The Extrude Along Path option will sweep a closed shape along a path direction.

Shape   path

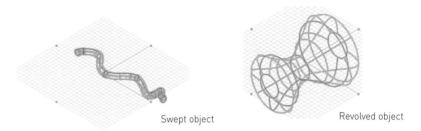

Swept object   Revolved object

COPY/ARRAY

Often in CAD, modelling objects are repeated – steps for a staircase are one such example. It would be tedious to model each step individually and assemble them. This is where the Copy, Repeat Copy and Array commands come into their own.

Each software interface has different methods of executing the command. Typically the Array command is used to perform multiple copies, while Copy is used for just one or two copies. The Copy command is also sometimes known as Duplicate.

Above
A single object has been multiplied, rotated and scaled at set incremental stages.

Below
In this example a single house has been duplicated by using the Array tool to create a terrace of houses.

TIP KEY COMMANDS

Use the keyboard commands:
ARRAY/3DARRAY. Co = COPY

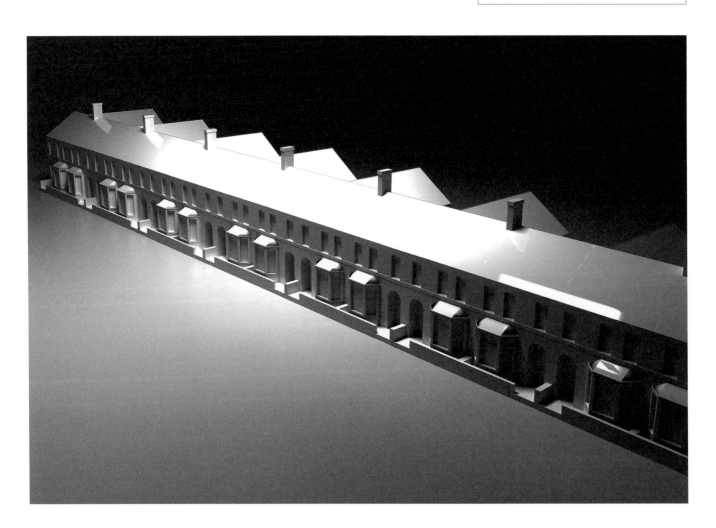

AutoCAD

COPY

You can create a single copy by simply using the Cmd + C (mac)/Ctrl + C (pc) shortcut and using the Paste (Cmd + V/Ctrl + V) keyboard option. Use the 2D Copy option to do simple singular or multiple copies of an object.

 Copy

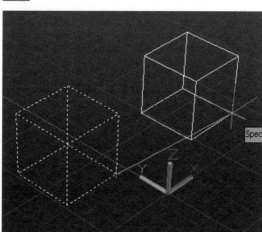

ARRAY

Array has changed dramatically in AutoCAD 2012. It still follows the same principles of the type – rectangular, polar, etc., and the specification of the number of columns and rows needed. The input window has gone, however, and now all the information is entered on screen or through the command line.

 Array

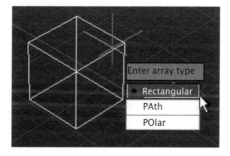

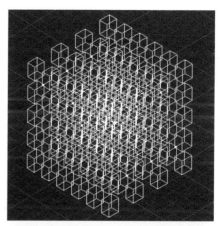

- Select object to array
- Enter type (Rectangle, Polar)
- Number of rows
- Number of columns
- Number of levels
- Specify distance between row/column levels

When creating an array there can be at least eight different levels of data required. If you create a simple array in 2D or 3D you can use the Properties command to post edit the array (e.g. increase or decrease the number of columns, rows, objects, etc.).

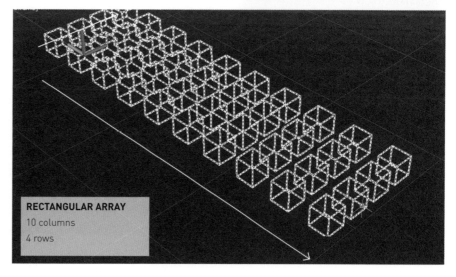

RECTANGULAR ARRAY
10 columns
4 rows

3ds Max

COPY/EDIT/CLONE

You can create a single copy in 3ds Max by simply using the copy, Cmd + C (mac)/Ctrl + C (pc), shortcut and the paste (Cmd + V/Ctrl + V) keyboard option. Clone will give you more options, allowing you to make the object an 'instance' so it becomes linked to the object that you copied.

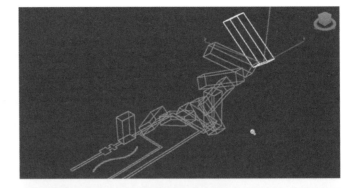

To create this image, the options shown below were selected.

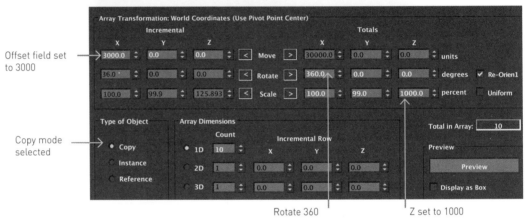

Offset field set to 3000

Copy mode selected

Rotate 360

Z set to 1000

Maya

SINGLE COPY MODE

You can create a single copy in Maya by simply using the copy and paste keyboard shortcuts. Duplicate will give you more options, allowing you to make the object an 'instance' so it becomes linked to the object that you copied.

ARRAY

In Maya Duplicate Special is the equivalent of Array. In the examples here I have first copied 10 times in a column direction and then selected the objects and copied them again 10 times in a row. You also have the option of Rotate and Scale. The box icon is selected so the tool can be applied as many times as needed.

Copy offset on X axis

10 copies

Copy offset on Z axis

10 copies

Form Z

COPY

You can create a single copy in Form Z by using the copy and paste keyboard shortcuts. The Form Z Move tool set has many levels, from singular to macro moves.

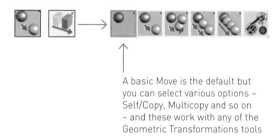

A basic Move is the default but you can select various options – Self/Copy, Multicopy and so on – and these work with any of the Geometric Transformations tools

ARRAY

Array is performed by the Multicopy command. In this example a single block has been copied 12 times; the Copy mode was set to automatically repeat. The use of endpoint snap along with accurate placement creates the steps.

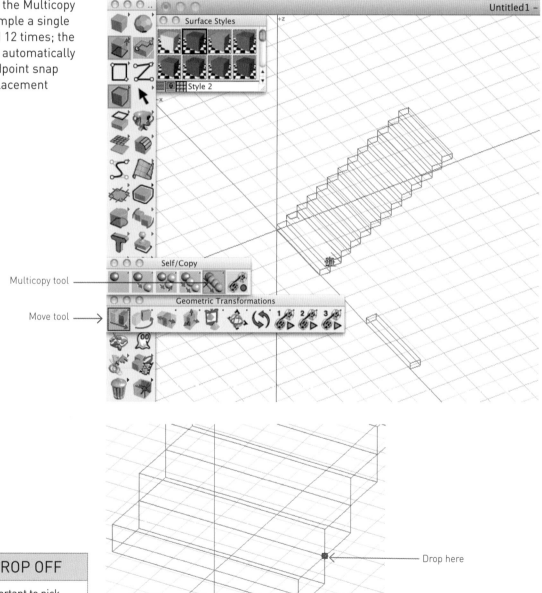

Multicopy tool

Move tool

Drop here

Pick here

SketchUp

COPY

You can create a single copy in SketchUp by simply using the cut and paste keyboard shortcuts.

Selecting the Move tool and using the Ctrl (mac)/Alt (pc) option will allow you to create a copy of an object and place it accurately. This tool also performs the array function.

 Move

Using the Alt (mac)/ Ctrl (pc) option brings up the + sign for Copy mode

ARRAY

An array in SketchUp is reliant on the Copy tool. You can first enter an offset distance for a single copy. While the copy is selected and after the Move is completed you can enter a multiple value in the length field, such as x10.

Using the Alt (mac)/Ctrl (pc) command activate the Move tool to copy and array.

While still selected (after the move) the value x10 was entered into the data field

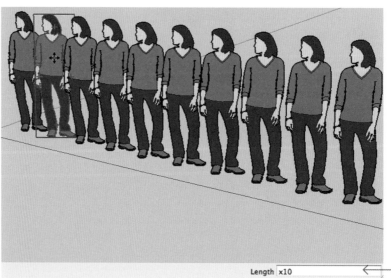

Length x10

Vectorworks

COPY

In Vectorworks you can use the Cmd + C (mac)/Ctl + C (pc) keys to copy any object in a scene. Duplicate will give you more options, such as creating and instancing an object.

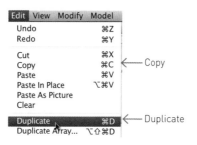

Single copy move tool

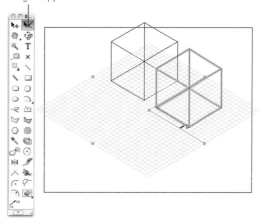

ARRAY

Duplicate Array allows you to create an array of objects in the XY and Z directions. You can also scale and rotate the objects in the array.

The array arrangement can be linear in a row, rectangular in rows and columns, or circular (polar).

In this example a single cube has been copied in a rectangular array with three rows and three columns. The distance between copies is the same as the object – 3000mm.

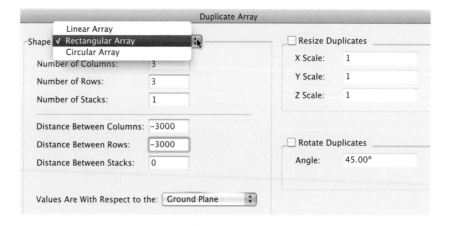

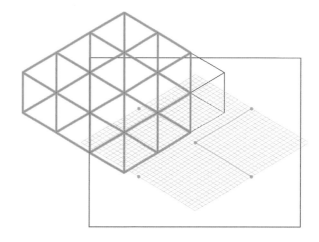

TUTORIAL 2 3D EXERCISE: MODEL MESH AND ADVANCED CREATE

This 3D exercise will introduce the key tools that have been discussed in the 3D modelling section. When you feel you have gained enough confidence to move on to the next stage do so, but, as mentioned with the previous tutorial, do not avoid trying the same section again if you need more practise to master the basic commands. Repetition is crucial for building your confidence and skills.

The exercise is generic to all the software covered in this section. You will need to apply the correct type of tool for each section, and there can often be more than one option. A useful exercise would be to try out the different options to gain experience in any specific software.

Some smaller, simplified exercises are the Mesh, Sweep and Revolve sections. You may want to apply these as contextual objects in the shop model.

NOTE: Remember to save your file regularly throughout the exercise.

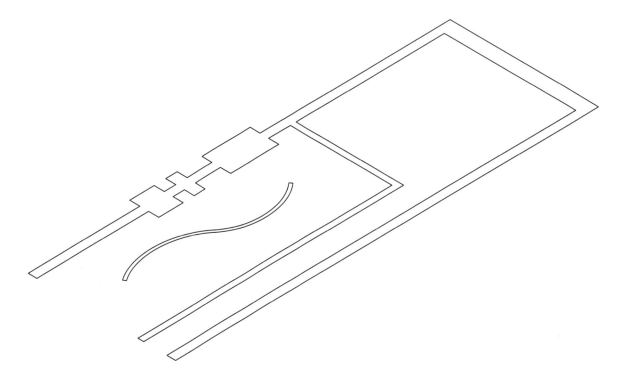

Import the shop plan and set the view to Iso/Axo

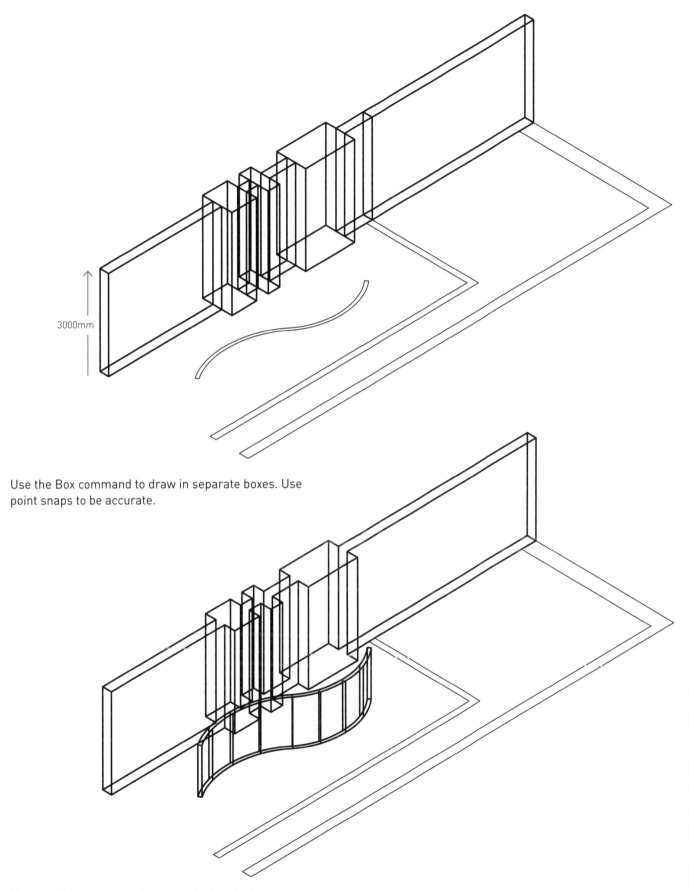

3000mm

Use the Box command to draw in separate boxes. Use
point snaps to be accurate.

Use the Union command to group/union the boxes

Use Presspull or Extrude to create a curved screen

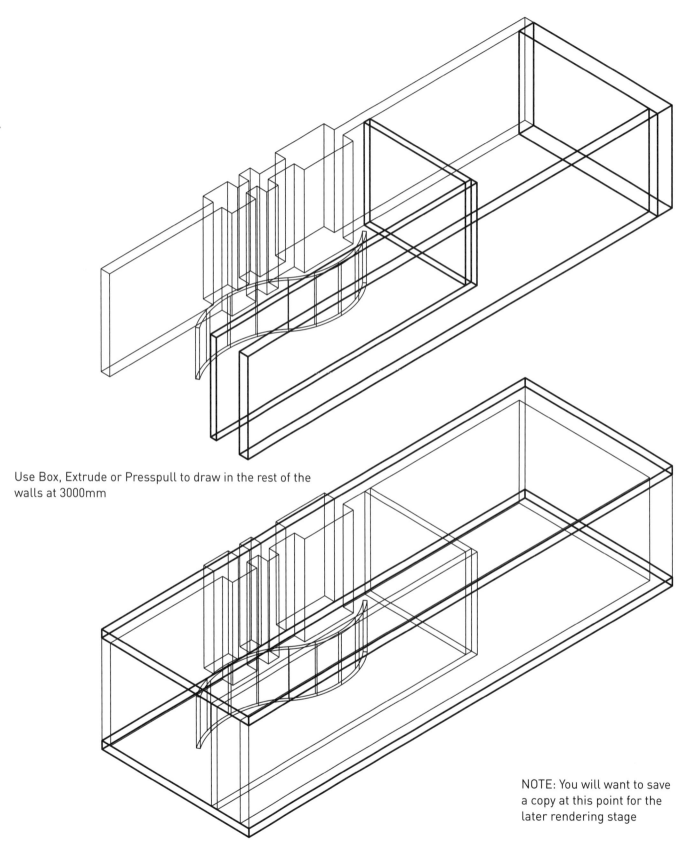

Use Box, Extrude or Presspull to draw in the rest of the
walls at 3000mm

NOTE: You will want to save
a copy at this point for the
later rendering stage

Using Box and Endpoints, draw in a ceiling and floor plane
using a box to a height of 250mm

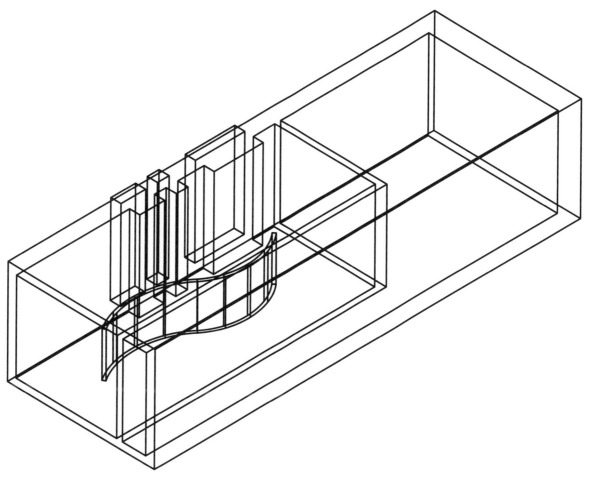

Select all and use the Union command (or Group) to make one object

NOTE: Linework is now continuous

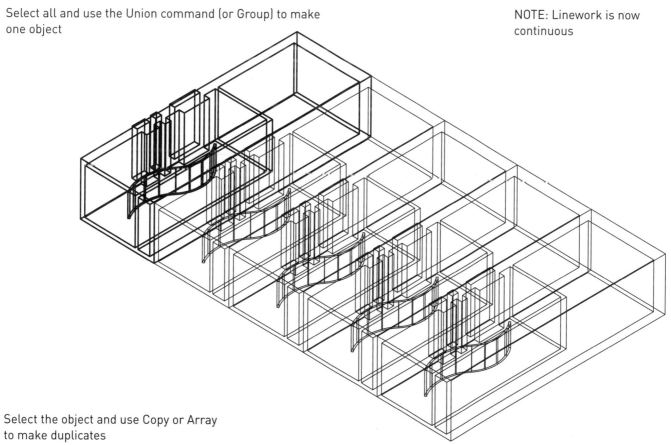

Select the object and use Copy or Array to make duplicates

PART 3 RENDERING

RENDERING BASICS

If any part of the CAD process has become irreplaceable it is the perspective and visualization capabilities of CAD. We can now simulate and test the aesthetic qualities of our design, in some cases in real time. We shouldn't look at this media in isolation; the aesthetic skills acquired in sketching and rendering tone and colour into a drawing are important.

Artistic skill cannot be developed purely on the computer – you often see the evidence of this in computer visualizations. Remember that photo realization is not necessarily the end game; evoking the mood and atmosphere is equally important.

Camera perspectives

Following the completion, or even during the development of a design, you can get into the model with a camera and see the environment in set perspective parameters. Gone are the days when you would set up a perspective grid and either use the measured or judgement method to construct a perspective representation. That's not to say that the days of hand-drawn sketch perspectives are redundant; they do still form an important part of the design process. However, many hours are saved from the ability to track around a model to find the 'right' view.

Above
Dutch architects MVRDV have for some time been harnessing computer renderings to communicate complex proposals. Shown here is their winning entry in the competition to design the new town of Gwanggyo in Korea (top) and their research project exploring urban farming (above).

Below
A CAD 3D model of a typical street. The camera allows you to navigate and select endless perspective views.

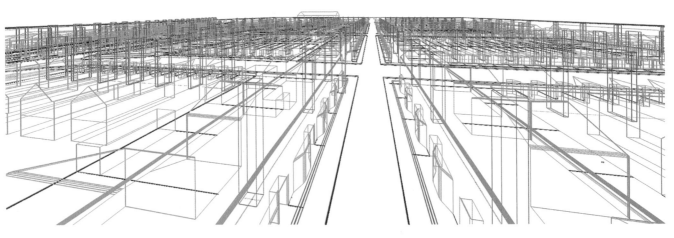

Material and light

The ability to add material and lighting to a model is now at a photorealistic stage. For architects, interior designers and clients this provides a wonderful opportunity to be specific about material and lighting choices. Sketch rendering is very important in the design process but the ability to check how one material reads with another is invaluable. In lighting terms it is now possible to track how sunlight enters a built structure accurately and in real time. These models are having a significant influence on the design process of contemporary building.

Rendering

Although perspective is key, rendering is equally important to all the views available in the architectural palette. Isometric views or a rendered section help to describe a design more accurately. The process of rendering follows a similar format in all CAD programs, although you will have different settings to give you different quality results. The basics of the render interface have changed little in 30 years but it has evolved to become more accurate and, to a certain extent, more complex. The way that game rendering has moved from Atari's Pong to the current Xbox LIVE experience is just one example of how far it has developed.

Output

In rendering, resolution issues are often ignored, which can lead to problems both in production and realization. In the early stages of image production a reverse principle applies – you should keep the resolution of your image at a low level; quick updates of a view are invaluable when developing the composition of a render.

However, at later stages, an image that is of a low resolution often has limited use. If you work on the principle of outputting any image at the maximum quality you can attain (within reason) you will be able to use it at different print sizes. Other settings within the render environment will also be discussed here, which will allow you to tweak visual outputs, making them crisper or more detailed.

Right
A rendered CAD perspective, with materials, lights and environment added to the model.

Working render settings

There have been major advancements in rendering over the past 30 years. When modelling, the visual settings can be changed from wire line to surface with shadows, etc. These basic settings are very useful when setting up a perspective view as it can sometimes be difficult to assess the view in wireframe mode.

All software will have the ability to move through the visual settings. Interactive, shaded surface and wire line are the basic rendered representations of your model and they all work in real time and update instantly.

Setting up the camera

Most camera settings are the same; to insert a camera to a view you would normally specify the start and end point of the camera view (cone). Many additional settings will be similar to a physical camera, such as the use of a 35mm lens setting. Quite often a perspective can be skewed or unnatural when the camera settings are tampered with. In general you will be looking to create a perspective view that is natural, or as you would see in a human perspective, although there are exceptions where artistic licence might be called for.

In the 3D modelling environment you can also use the set orthographic views to help you navigate a model. You can set most camera views up with orthographic projection (straight lines) – this is useful as sometimes the three-point perspective view can look a little wonky.

Whatever settings you use for a camera, its power comes from being able to set a view that you can work up. Often you will accidentally hit a good view when navigating a model, only to lose it again as you carry on. Every time you add a camera view you will be able to easily return back to it.

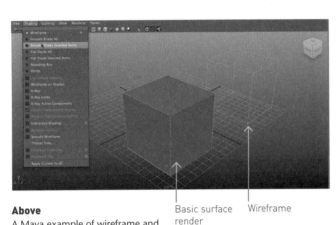

Above
A Maya example of wireframe and a shaded surface.

Basic surface render   Wireframe

TIP WIREFRAME MODE

If your model is very complicated you may want to switch from Shaded to Wireframe mode when you navigate your model, as it can be a very processor-intensive activity to be in interactive mode.

Below left
A 3ds Max target camera inserted in plan view to get the correct direction and length.

Below
The camera view is selected to show the basic perspective view. You can easily return to default view.

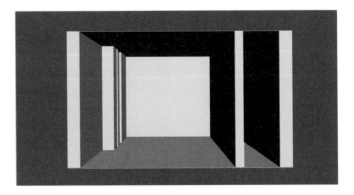

Setting/fixing the view

Often when setting a view it can look perfect in wireframe but when you come to do an initial render you can be inside a wall or object resulting in a blank screen. Use interactive render to check the view and adjust accordingly. Interactive render may be the best setting to track around your model as it gives you a good representation of surface and form.

When setting up interior views it may help to delete the odd wall or column so they don't get in the way of the view. While this may not be a true view, a bit of artistic licence can be practical when trying to set up a perspective of your scheme.

When dealing with very complex models the creation of a computer model to view can be very beneficial in render terms. More often than not I set up a scene as a stage set, deleting everything I cannot see in the view. You effectively keep all the elements contained in the view; this is equally useful for the facade of an architectural building – deleting all the interior elements. While the computer may not be rendering the elements, it often spends time working out the rendering of hidden objects.

As a working methodology you may well choose to have a file per view. So you will have multiple files, each with a singular view where the contents reflect the view you wish to render. For less complex models you will have all the views and the complete model. While this is not standard practice, it can effectively speed up the rendering process, and any increase in rendering speed is always a good thing.

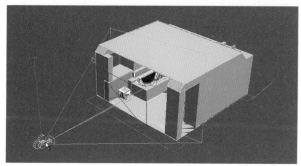

Above
This view of a bathroom interior allows you to see the bathroom in its entirety. The wall has been removed in the model below to allow a complete view to be taken.

TIP PERSPECTIVE

Try to keep your view natural. It is often tempting to add a lot of depth and foreshortening to a perspective, yet a typical eye view is usually the best choice, since this gives a true representation of what a design would look like in real life.

There are exceptions to this rule. The visual here does use depth and foreshortening for a more dynamic effect, but take care – this is very easily overdone.

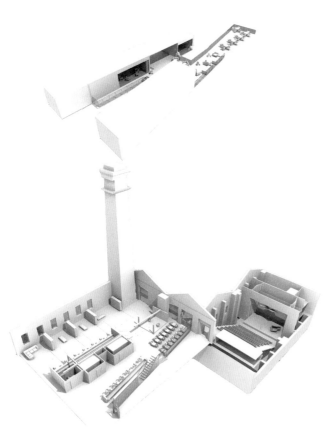

Turn it white

Once you have set a view for render development then the first material you could apply is a simple white material. This is really useful for accessing the form, composition and tonal qualities of a model. When you are dealing with glass and transparent materials it is useful to define these with a simple glass material or even a simple transparent white material. The simplification of the model material is often reminiscent of a physical design model you would create by hand.

The two examples shown here demonstrate the usefulness of leaving a scheme model white – the design can be viewed easily. The inclusion of materials at this scale can often give a 'doll's house effect'.

Above
An exploded axonometric rendered with a simple white material to express the 3D forms of the scheme.

Right
A mass model of an urban site, the colour elements serve to describe the design elements of the scheme.

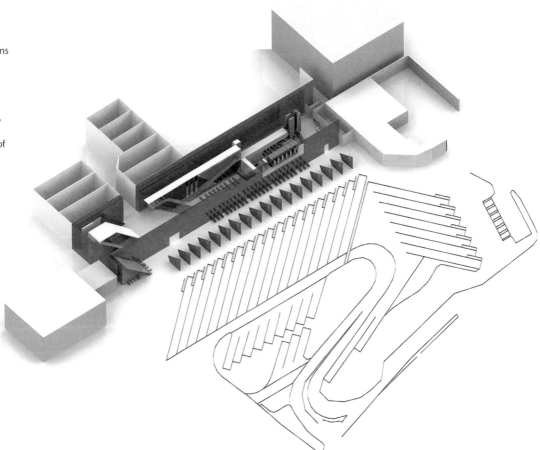

Light

Less is more; nothing slows down a 3D rendering more than improper use of lighting. Computers and 3D software are good these days, and if you have a really good computer then you may well be able to simulate every light fitting in an exterior or interior model. But why would you do this when one correctly positioned light will probably give you the desired results and a lot less trouble than trying to sync 20 sets of lights?

Light without shadows can also be a pointless exercise, and can lead to the flat overexposure of an image. Aesthetically, depth and tone are as important as the need for light in a scene. Daylight, in particular, is an important consideration for any exterior or interior visual. If you look around in real life you will see that shadows created by natural and artificial light are never uniform, thus creating depth.

Some core principles exist for lighting a scene, then. Ensure that you use the minimal amount of lighting needed in a scheme and your file should perform well. Make sure, too, that you have your shadows turned on (you can turn troublesome ones off) to emphasize depth and the surface of form.

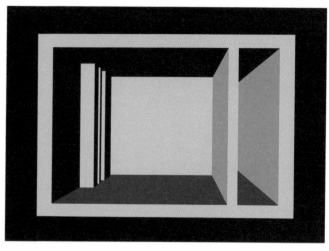

Interior point light

Exterior point light

Above
A basic render in Form Z of the shop model, with the default ambient light and no shadows.

Left
Adding two point lights to the model scene with shadows on adds depth and tone to the image.

Left
A simple CAD perspective of the shop model, white material with a basic lighting setup.

Materials

The default material in all 3D programs is normally a simple colour with a matt reflective finish, often referred to as a 'shader' or 'texture'. You will see names such as 'Blinn' and 'Phong' in some of the advanced rendering programs as material types – these actually come from the names of the people who invented them. Jim Blinn invented the Blinn shader in the early 1970s, and it is still being used by programs today.

Materials assigned to 3D objects contain many properties, of which colour is only one. You can add reflection, images, bumps, displacements and many more attributes. Of all the attributes available, the ability to add real images to a 3D object can have profound effect on the visual complexity of a perspective image. Images used in

TIP MATERIAL IMAGES

Take your own images of materials to add a realistic feel to your work.

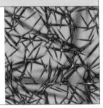

Colour map

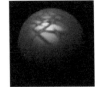

Specular

Bump

Transparency

Reflectivity

Displacement

A predefined material from the architecture and design templates in 3ds Max, rendered in Mental Ray.

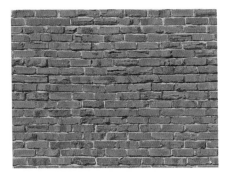

A texture map of a brick wall from a photograph. The image is prepared ready to be repeated (tiled).

The brick texture map applied to a sphere rendered in 3ds Max with the Vray plug-in.

Final render settings

Type of renderer

By default nearly all programs will have a basic render setup as a default. This is fine as it lets you quickly develop a model or image to a suitable level. When it comes to a final production render you will need to modify the settings and in some cases actually change the type of render engine that you have been using. Overall you want the maximum quality of image processing that you can attain. This is often dictated by how fast your CPU is and how much RAM you have in your computer.

GI/Final Gather

In recent years Global Illumination has been included in most render interfaces, even within SketchUp plug-ins. GI gives you soft, warm shadows, accurately computing the light reflection on surfaces. GI will allow you to use properties such as self illumination, which is useful as an alternative light source. All this accuracy of computing secondary light fall does come at a price; it increases render times quite substantially. You can store the GI data so it can be reused or you can lower the levels of calculation so it performs faster. Final Gather is a method of economically computing global illumination and can also be found in most rendering interfaces. Global Illumination dramatically increases the visual aesthetic and accuracy of a final image, so it's best to use it for a final rendered image.

Render resolution

When you typically open up a 3D rendering program it will be set either to screen size or a set resolution such as 640 x 480 dpi, or even as low as 320 x 240 which are typically good resolutions to work a visualization up with. The 320 x 240 setting is particularly useful if things are really starting to slow down.

If you intend to print an image at, say, A4 on a 300dpi printer then the resolution you would need as a image output is going to be 2480 x 3508! You may get away with less as it will take quite some time to render (could be days) but there is one rule in resolution: you cannot increase the resolution of an image once it is complete.

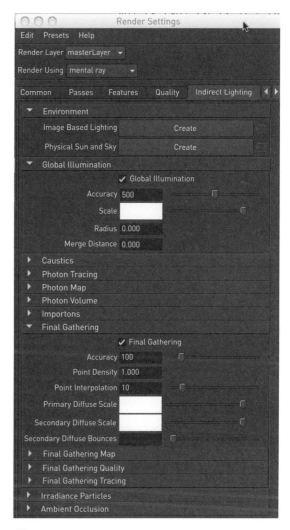

Above
The Render Settings dialogue: Global Illumination and Final Gathering settings in Maya.

Below
The Image Size dialogue in AutoCAD; note the option to specify your own image size, which is useful for increasing the resolution of a final render.

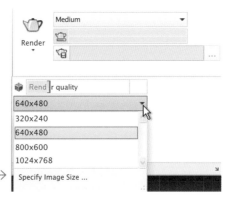

Specify Image Size

AutoCAD rendering

1: INTERFACE

There are many different environments that you can adopt when creating renders in AutoCAD. The 3D modelling environment is the default for rendering with a tab's interface.

As has been introduced in the drawing and modelling sections, you could opt for the Classic interface and use the right-click functionality to open the very same toolbars. Either interface is fine, they both do the same job. But the AutoCAD Classic interface, along with some simple keyboard shortcuts, is a failsafe interface. When rendering you will use only two of the tab sections, Render and View.

THE 3D MODELLING ENVIRONMENT

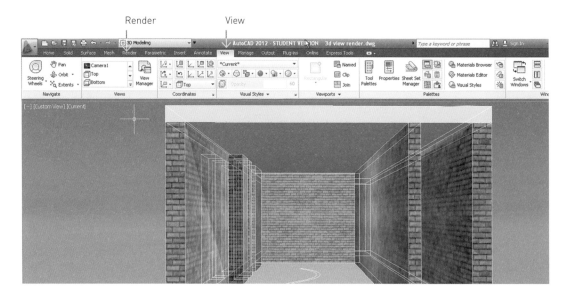

VIEW TAB
The View environment allows you to add a camera, set the surface style, etc.

RENDER TAB
The Render tab contains all the tools needed to add lights, materials and output an visualization.

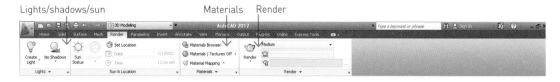

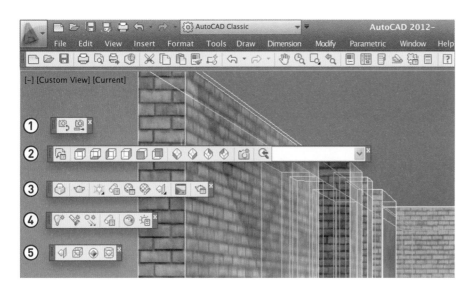

① Camera Adjust
② View
③ Render
④ Lights
⑤ Mapping

All the tools discussed in this section are contained in the View – the Render, Lights and Mapping toolbars.

AUTOCAD CLASSIC

View with the toolbars opened with the right-click function.

2: CAMERA

Note: The Camera tool should be located in the ribbon bar/view.

AutoCAD has a habit of moving tools around an interface and it is for that reason that the command line is your friend.

The command line entry to activate the camera tool is CAMERA. It is a simple click-and-point operation and is best placed in plan.

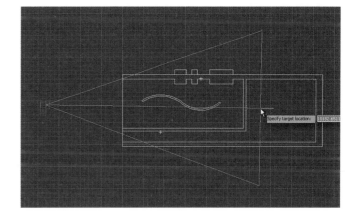

AUTOCAD CLASSIC

If you are using the Classic interface the camera can be found in the View toolbar.

After inserting the camera, when you click on the camera icon a camera preview will appear. From this pane you can also set the visual style of the camera view.

You can further set the height parameter to eye height – 1600mm – by using the Properties palette, along with many other options, such as field of view.

Camera Preview

Camera height set to 1600mm

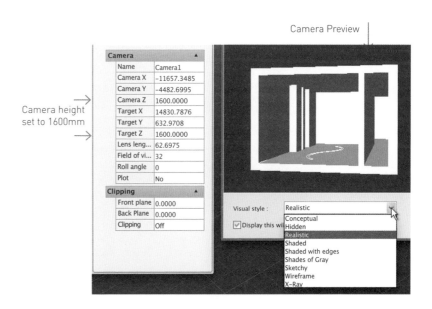

CAMERA VIEW

You can reference the Camera view through various methods. If you are using the 3D modelling environment you can either use the View box or you can use the view environment in the workspace.

AUTOCAD CLASSIC

You can find the Camera view in the toolbar.

Camera view can be selected here

Camera view can also be selected here

Camera view

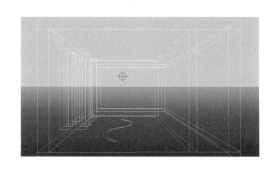

When the Camera view is selected it will be displayed on the working screen

3: LIGHT AND BACKGROUND

Adding a light is a very simple procedure – you use the light ribbon to add a point light to the scene.

Create Light

You can select the ribbon icon or if you are in Classic then the Lights toolbar will add a point light by default.

The other option is to use the command line entry LIGHT and choose a point light.

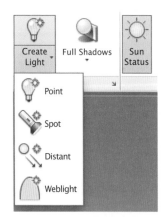

AUTOCAD CLASSIC

Point   Light Lister

DEFAULT SETTINGS

In all cases you will be met with an option to turn default lighting off. As you want the scene lit by the lights you specify, then you should opt to do this.

By default the lighting units are not set to suitable lighting units. You may not see the effect of your light on the scene. Set the units to Generic and you will soon see the effect.

Generic lighting

SUNLIGHT AND SHADOWS

To add a bit of realism to your lighting you can use AutoCAD's Sky Background and Illumination setting. You can also set the scene to have Full Shadows. This setup takes full advantage of the Global Illumination and Final Gather.

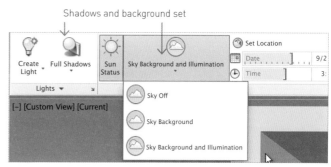

Shadows and background set

LIGHT LEVEL ADJUSTMENTS

You will want to see how the lights you have added affect the scene, so a quick test render will be useful.

You can access the light settings by selecting the light and using the PROP keyboard command to bring up the properties of the light. Use the command line to activate the Render window (RENDER) and to bring up light properties (PROP).

AUTOCAD CLASSIC

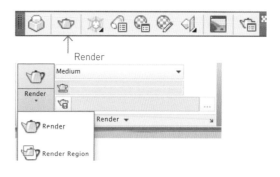

Render

Command line
• CAMERA
• LIGHT (SELECT OPTIONS)
• LIGHT LIST
• RENDER

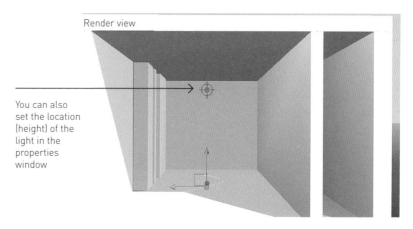

Render view

You can also set the location (height) of the light in the properties window

4: MATERIALS

TURN IT WHITE

You will see in the previous render preview that the default material for AutoCAD is white.

As with most rendering programs you need to enable the view of materials/textures so they can be seen in the viewport as well as the final render.

Note: This can also be activated by typing VSMATERIALMODE in the command line and selecting 2.

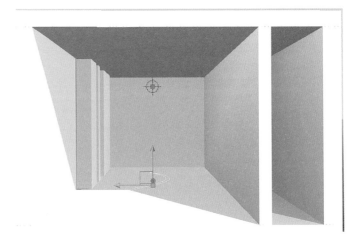

View textures

CREATING A NEW MATERIAL

You can use the Material Browser to apply an existing predefined material, such as metal or glass. If you double click the material it opens up the Material Editor, which allows you to alter existing Material properties.

AUTOCAD CLASSIC

If you are using the Classic interface, you can select Material Options in the Render toolbar.

Material Options

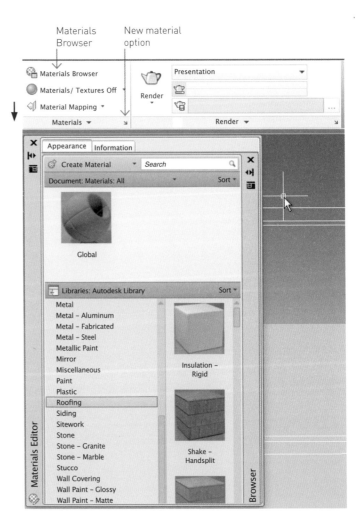

Materials Browser

New material option

① To create a new material double click the Global Material icon to activate the Material Editor.

② Use the image slot to add a texture map.

③ Use the Scale option to tile the texture

④ Name your new texture

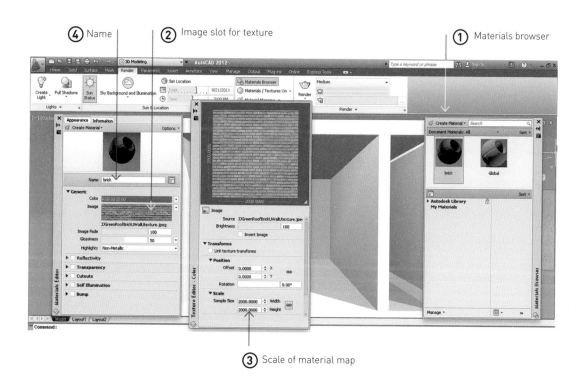

④ Name | **②** Image slot for texture | **①** Materials browser

③ Scale of material map

TEXTURE MAPPING

While you cannot tile with the texture mapping option you can select the type of mapping. Box and Planar are the typical settings that you would use.

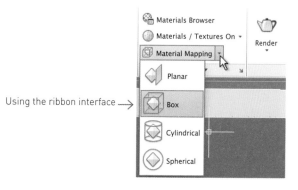

Using the ribbon interface →

AUTOCAD CLASSIC
Texture mapping option toolbar

APPLY A MATERIAL

A material can be added to a scene easily using a simple drag and drop action.

BACKGROUND

You can use the View Manager to set an image background. Available in the window pane or under the View menu. You will need to have created a named view such as a camera. Select the general properties of the view, select the Background Override option and load a suitable image. When rendered the image will be in the background.

Drag and drop

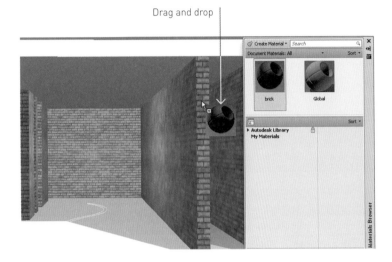

Select background override and set your image

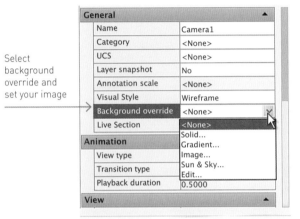

RENDER A REGION

As you have already experienced, before you can use the Render option to see the view rendered, you can also use the Render Region option to render the window view.

When you render you will most likely need to adjust the lighting parameters. It is useful to keep the Light Lister (Lights in Model) open. You can also do this by selecting the light and double clicking to bring up the properties (or select and type PROP).

Click here to open the Light Lister

The Render Region option

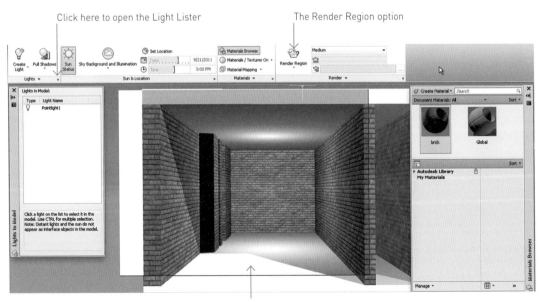

This area has been rendered

5: FINAL RENDER SETTINGS

You can alter the final quality of the render using the Render Presets options in the ribbon bar.

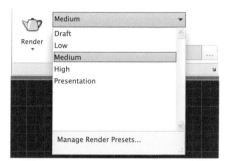
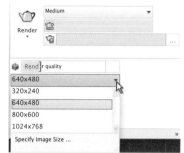

You can also set the image size through this dialogue

A simple view with concrete and wooden floor rendered in Presentation mode

ADVANCED RENDER PALETTE

By far the easiest way to set the final render options is to open the Advanced Render Settings palette. This can be easily activated by typing RPREF into the command line. It will give you image size options as well as a chance to tinker with the Global Illumination and Final Gather settings.

FILE SAVE

You can use the File Save option to save the image file in a suitable format such as tiff, jpeg, etc. You can also right click on the render job to select this.

If you want to save the Render Region view, e.g. part wireframe, part rendered, then use the keyboard command SAVE IMG.

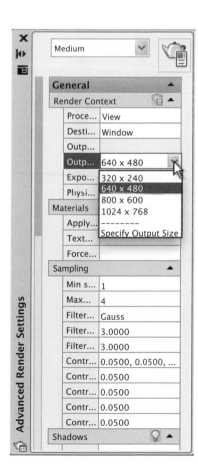
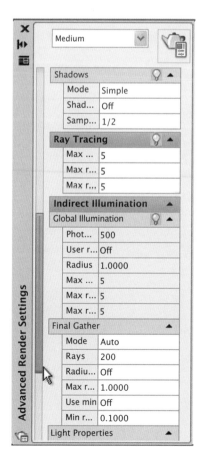

3DS MAX rendering

1 : INTERFACE

3ds Max is a wonderfully intuitive rendering program – the interface is set up to facilitate rendering. When modelling or importing a model you will want to change a few settings for an effective render environment.

The default render engine for 3ds Max is Scanline Render but I prefer to use Mental Ray (MR) as it gives full GI and Final Gather, as well as a series of specialist materials such as Architecture and Design.

I will demonstrate this at the start up so I can use MR in the development of the visual and not just at the final render.

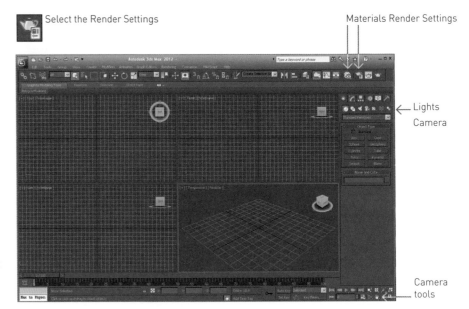

Select the Render Settings

Materials Render Settings

Lights
Camera

Camera tools

The Render Settings will open and you will note that the setting is Default Scanline Render. This is quite an extensive palette. You will need to move from one part to the other using the scroll bar.

(1) In the Common tab, scroll down to Choose Renderer.

(2) Select the Choose Renderer field, click on the box option and a pop-up will appear.

(3) Select Mental Ray.

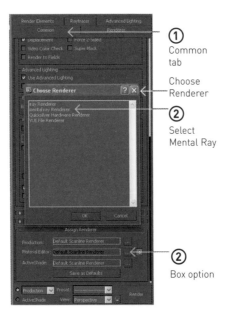

(1) Common tab

Choose Renderer

(2) Select Mental Ray

(2) Box option

Indirect illumination tab

Final Gather render settings (keep low)

(2)

Caustics and GI settings

When the Render Settings window changes to Mental Ray you will see that an Indirect Illumination tab appears. The option to select GI is in this field; Final Gather is already activated by default .

It is good practice to change this setting at the very beginning

2: CAMERA

INSERT CAMERA

It is best to insert the camera in plan view, but with other software it's probably best to adjust the view with the excellent camera tools available in 3ds Max.

The Camera tools are based in the Create tab of the command panel. The default is Object Creation. You will need to select the Camera icon and then the type of camera you need; in this case a Target Camera is best as it allows you to specify two points.

You can select the camera view by using the View panel by selecting View › Cameras.

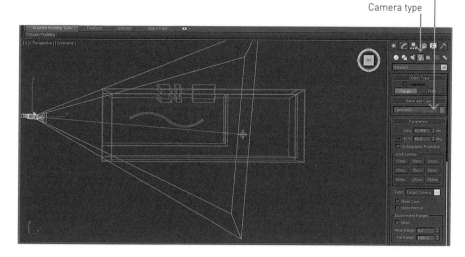

Camera creation
Camera type

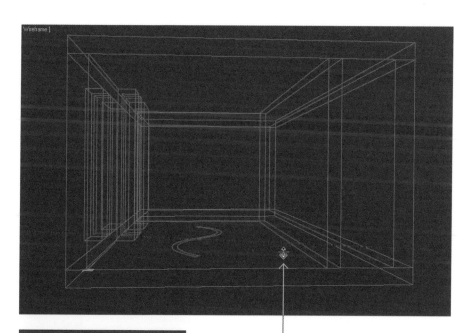

Use the excellent Camera tools, such as Pan Dolly, to help you adjust and create the view you require. Since you have set up as a camera any adjustments will be saved.

A camera view being modified using the Dolly tool to zoom in and out

VIEW MATERIAL

You can easily switch between wireframe and realistic render by using the View pane.

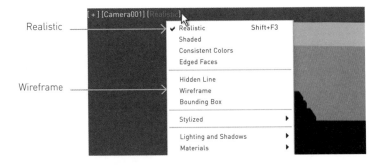

Realistic

Wireframe

TURN WHITE

This software program has a habit of using a new colour for each object you create, which is useful when modelling. When rendering, however, it's best to neutralize these materials to white – the default grey/white material ('Blinn') is fine.

So before we introduce lights we need to access the Material Editor. You can invoke this via the icon in the Render section or preferably (as you will be opening and closing it quite a bit) via the keyboard shortcut M.

A Slate Material Editor has recently been introduced to the 3ds Max interface. In previous versions there was only the option of the Compact Material Editor. I personally prefer the latter, but you can use either – both will do the job.

Material Editor

Slate Material Editor option

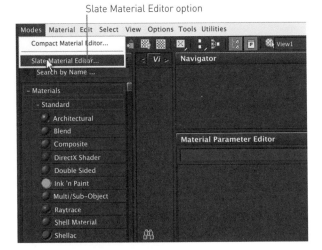

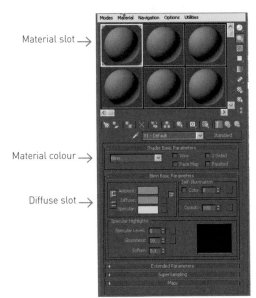

Material slot →

Material colour →

Diffuse slot →

LEFT
The colour and the tone of a material is based in the diffuse slot.

BELOW
You can simply drag and drop the material into the scene.

3: LIGHTS AND BACKGROUND

Lights are located next to the Camera tool in the Create tab.

By default 3ds Max starts up with photometric lights and as you will be using Mental Ray (MR) to render you will prefer to use standard lights. You will need to use the drop-down menu to switch to these.

In this lighting setup I have used two MR area omni lights, one inside one out, and a skylight, which has been placed randomly in the view.

Under the visual style, Realistic has been activated and you can instantly see changes appear as the lights are added or moved.

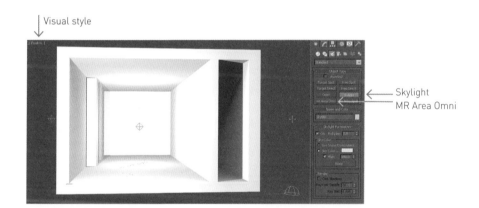

Render

After adding your lights it would be a good idea to do a test render of the view to check that the settings are good.

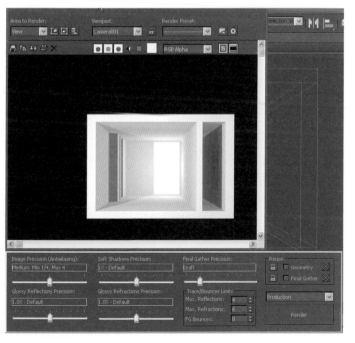

TEST RENDER PREVIEW
You may want to move the slide settings to draft/low so it speeds along.

LIGHTING ADJUSTMENTS

There is a useful tool in 3ds Max to adjust the light settings: it's called the Light Lister and lists all the lights in the scene. From here you can easily adjust the light parameters.

Tools › Light Lister.

Light intensity

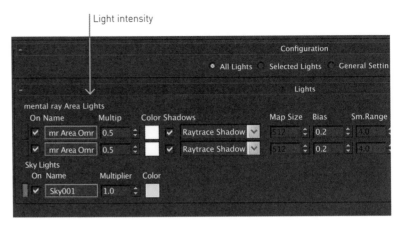

The Light Lister dialogue allows you to tweak the light settings

ADDING A BACKGROUND ENVIRONMENT

You can add an image to the background, which is useful in setting the perspective when dealing with a specific context. If it is used as an environment map reflections and refractions will appear in reflective surfaces, further adding to the realism of the render.

You can add a image to a final render by selecting Rendering › Environment. The image will also be used in the render environment in reflective surfaces.

You can simply add an image to a working perspective by selecting View › Viewport Background

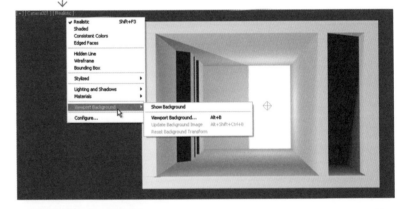

4 : MATERIALS

We have already introduced the
Material Editor in the section on light,
but you may also want to load textures
into the material slots.

To apply a texture to a material slot
you use the same diffuse slot but you
click the square icon to bring up a choice
of map type. In the case of images you
will want to load a bitmap, but this
can also be a jpeg or tiff format.

Select the Square in Diffuse

Pick Bitmap

Navigate to your image file

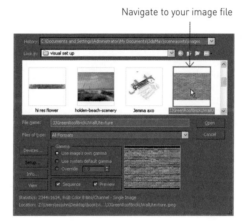

The loaded materials will be
shown in the Material Editor
(right). If you want them shown in
the working viewport you will have to
select Show Textures in the Viewport
option. This is very useful for tiling or
texture mapping.

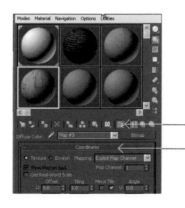

Show Textures in viewport

You will notice that the material
has moved to map coordinates.
While useful, this can also be
confusing. To go back to the base
material settings click on the
drop-down menu.

TEXTURE MAPPING

The UVW mapping option is located in the modifier tab and can be selected from the drop-down menu. The texture mapping capabilities in 3ds Max are very complex. These are used in gaming development. A texture map allows you to set the scale and position of the image file and tile it.

If an object is created in 3ds Max it will show the material assigned to it instantly. If it is imported from another program such as AutoCAD it will not show the texture until it has been texture mapped. The walls in this example were created in AutoCAD.

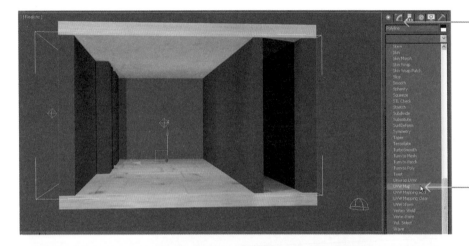

Modifier tab
The walls have been selected, the Modifier tab selected and a UVW map applied

UVW Map

After the UVW mapping has been applied then the box mapping option has been selected

The image map has also been tiled to become a more realistic scale (2 here)

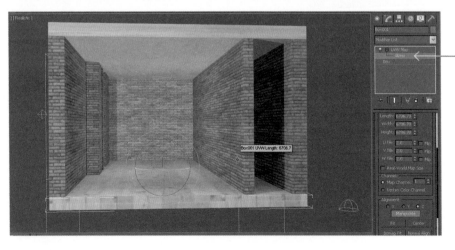

Here the orientation of the wooden floor map was incorrect. You can rotate, move, etc. a map using the Gizmo function and selecting the Rotate tool.

TIP UVW MAPPING

When using UVW mapping, the view updates instantly – it's interactive, so you are allowed a bit of trial and error.

5: FINAL RENDER SETTINGS

When producing a final render you will first need to go back to the image size settings. By default they are set to 640 x 480, which is fine for an image on the web, but you will want to increase the resolution for a final render. For this example I have increased the output to 2400 x 1800, which will be good to print at A4 or A3. When you do this it will add significantly to the render time.

In the Indirect Illumination tab there is a multitude of settings to work with. As you become more familiar with the software you may want to adjust these settings. Final Gather is on by default. Other options are available, such as Caustics, which is an advanced system for working out and displaying glass refraction.

NOTE: An object must be activated to display Caustics for this to happen.

A custom image res set to 2400 x 1800

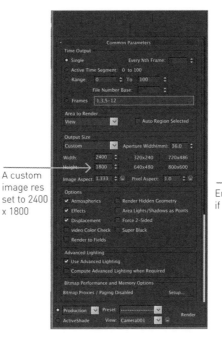

Enable GI if needed

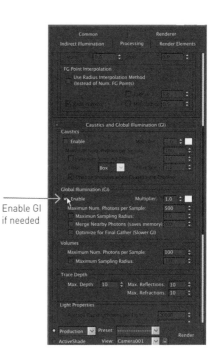

The Render window provides many functionality and tweaking possibilities.

There are many slide settings that you can use to improve your image. Image Precision (Antialiasing) is used to improve the detail being rendered, such as a brick bump map or any highly detailed element in the scene, but using it will add substantially to the render time.

Glossy reflections allow you to improve the reflections in a scene. Final Gather is an efficient algorithm for working out Global Illumination.

Once the render is completed you can save as an image format by selecting the floppy disk icon.

Floppy disk icon

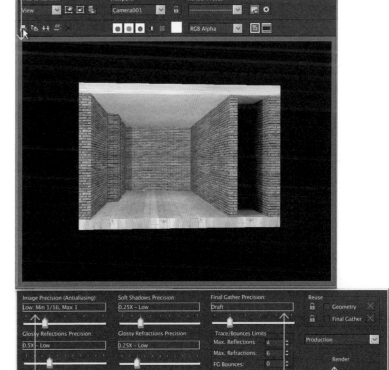

Increase Antialiasing

Final Gather settings

Invoke Render

Form Z rendering

1: INTERFACE

Form Z has an intuitive rendering environment; rendering takes place in the same window as the modelling environment. The interface is unique to Form Z so may seem a little alien, but the tools are quite simple to use.

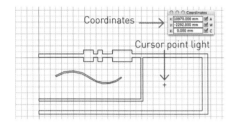

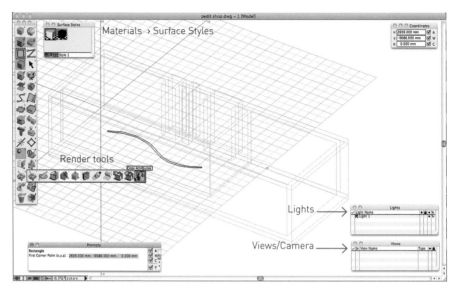

2: CAMERA

Form Z has a very different camera interface and no dedicated Camera tool. A view is loaded in the Views palette; you can then change that view to a camera type view.

It is useful to take sets of coordinates before you enter the Views palette – one set at the point where you would be standing and the other set at the view point.

The height coordinate is Z and is set to 1500mm in this example.

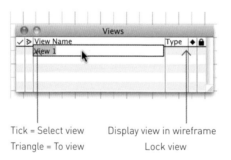

Tick = Select view
Triangle = To view
Display view in wireframe
Lock view

To create a view you need to double-click in the empty space in the Views palette.

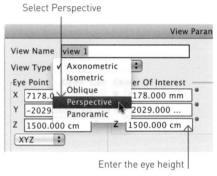

Enter the eye height

You then need to double-click the view you created to evoke the View dialogue. By default it will be set to a top view but you need to change it to perspective and enter the coordinates.

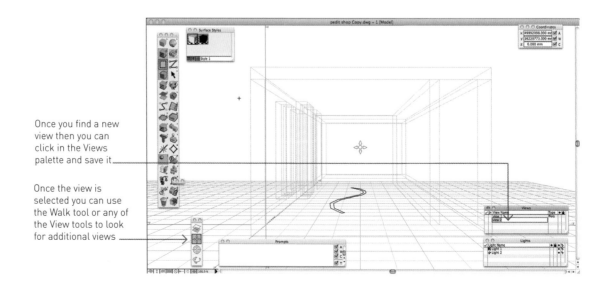

Once you find a new view then you can click in the Views palette and save it

Once the view is selected you can use the Walk tool or any of the View tools to look for additional views

TURN IT WHITE

In many cases the materials in the model are not likely to be white. You can use the Surface Style Parameters palette to change the colour of a material.

As with most of the Form Z dialogues, a double click on the Surface Styles palette will open up the option to change colour and associated parameters.

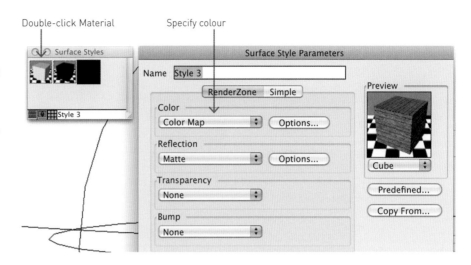

Double-click Material   Specify colour

3: LIGHTS AND BACKGROUND

To create a light you need to double-click in the empty space in the Lights palette.

If you double-click the newly created light you will bring up the Light Parameters dialogue. In this field you can set the location with coordinates and the type of light – a point light in this case.

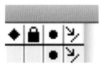

From left to right
Display/Lock/On Off/Shadows On Off

Point light   Location

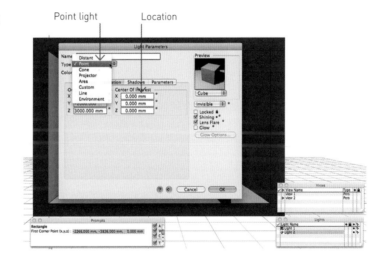

DISPLAY

You will want to see the perspective view with a surface material rather than in wireframe. Form Z has many display options – the default final render and most reliable render setting is called RenderZone: Display › RenderZone.

TIP SHORTCUTS

These keyboard shortcuts will allow you to toggle easily between wireframe and render modes.

Cmd (mac)/Ctrl (pc) + K = RenderZone
Cmd (mac)/Ctrl (pc) + W = Wireframe

Once you have added a point light you should go into Plan view as it is very easy to duplicate a light using the Copy mode, saving you from having to create a new light from scratch.

Using the Move/Copy tool to copy lights →

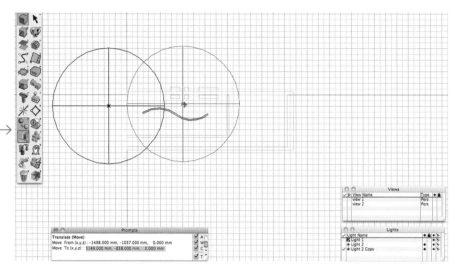

By setting the Tick icon next to your light you can use the Move tool to modify the location of the light. This can be useful when setting the sunlight direction.

Using the Move tool to adjust sunlight position

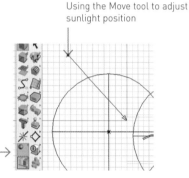

Using the Move tool to adjust light's position →

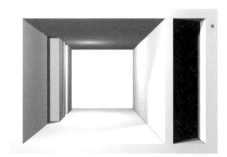

A simple white rendered view with two-point lights and sunlight

BACKGROUND

You can use the keyboard shortcut Cmd + U (mac)/ Ctl + U (pc) to activate the Underlay function. By using the Underlay and Wireframe mode you can set up a perspective view to relate to a background image

While Underlay will add an image to the viewport it won't be there for a final render, so you will also have to add the image as a background in RenderZone options.

Display › Display Options › RenderZone › RenderZone Options › Scene › Background › Background Map

4: MATERIALS

To add an image/texture to a new
material slot you first need to double-
click in the empty space to create
a new material. A Surface Styles
Parameters window will open. In the
Colour option use the drop-down
menu to select Colour Map.

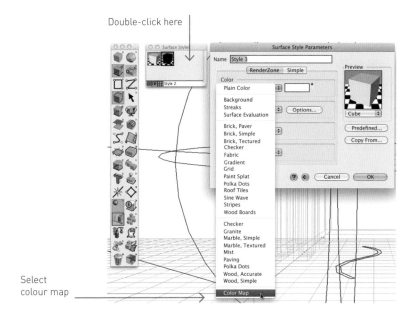

Double-click here

Select
colour map

LOAD AN IMAGE

Navigate to an image/texture map and
load; you will see the preview confirm
your selection.

There are also other options available
to you here – Reflection, Transparency
and Bump – and within these drop-
down menus there are many other
predefined maps that you can assign.

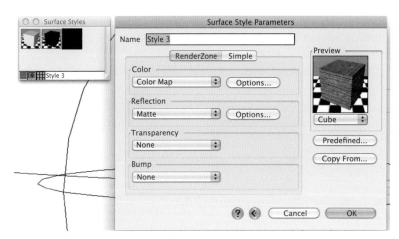

ASSIGN A MATERIAL

You will have to select the Colour
tool to assign a material to an object;
by default the material will not truly
assign unless you select the Clear
Surface option.

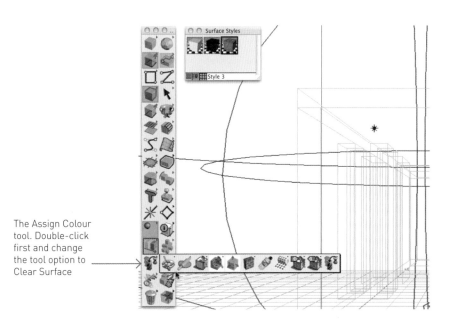

The Assign Colour
tool. Double-click
first and change
the tool option to
Clear Surface

TIP MATERIALS

Form Z also provides you with an
extensive set of predefined materials
such as glass, brick and grass.

TEXTURE MAP

By default it is unlikely that the assigned texture will be at a suitable scale. In this example you can see that the object has been tiled repetitively and is out of proportion. Use the Texture Map tool to format the texture's scale.

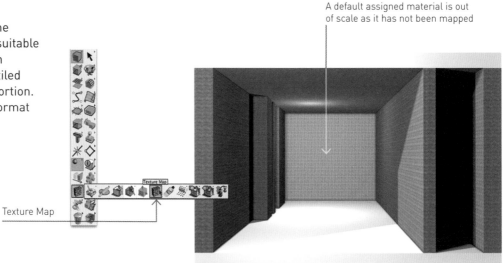

A default assigned material is out of scale as it has not been mapped

Texture Map

You can set the mapping type to planar, cylindrical, cubic as in other programs, and you can also set the size you want the image to be tiled at – in this case 2200mm.

A further drop-down menu will allow you to select the preview style.

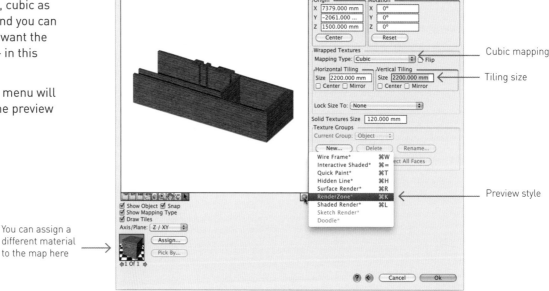

You can assign a different material to the map here

Cubic mapping

Tiling size

Preview style

If you have RenderZone selected you will automatically see the material updated to a realistic and appropriate scale.

Further adjustments may be made by clicking on the object with the Texture Map tool.

5: FINAL RENDER

As a final render you will want to increase the image size settings. I tend to work exclusively in RenderZone throughout the whole render development process as it can be quite quick at refreshing.

IMAGE OPTIONS

In the Image Options dialogue you can set the image size by size and resolution or by the number of pixels.

By Number of Pixels

By Scale and Resolution

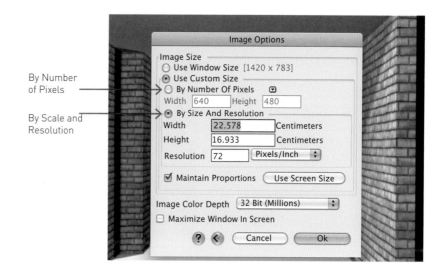

DISPLAY OPTIONS

There are many options in the Modelling Display Options, but as a final render you need to open the RenderZone selection. This also contains the GI settings.

Modelling Display Options

RenderZone Options

SAVE IMAGE

You can save the image in many formats by selecting File › Export Image.

Set Image Size allows you to render just a section of the image

GI settings

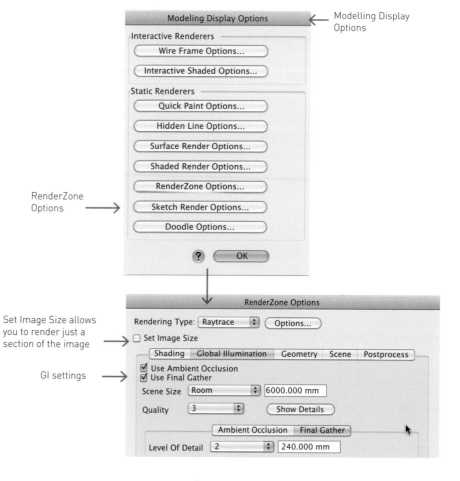

Maya rendering

1: INTERFACE

Maya is a complex rendering and animation program, with many levels. This section introduces some of the basic tools.

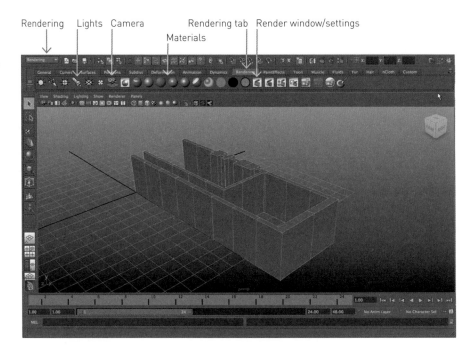

Rendering   Lights   Camera   Rendering tab   Render window/settings

Materials

It can be useful to set the Maya menu to Rendering and to select the Render tab as this contains nearly all the tools needed.

As with 3ds Max it can also be helpful to set the render option in Maya to Mental Ray, as MR allows you to use the GI feature, etc. You can open the Render Settings window by using an icon found in two different places.

Render Settings

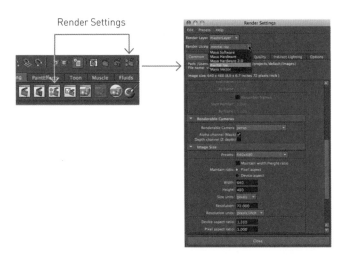

VIEWPORT SHADING

You can move between wireframe and shaded render types by selecting the shaded style from the window panes.

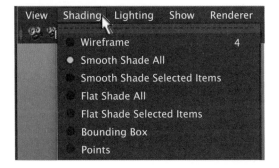

2 : CAMERA

There are a multitude of ways that you can create a camera in Maya; its animation core is based on this functionality. The simplest way of adding a target camera is to use the Camera and Aim option. This will allow you to modify the position and the view point. Go to Create › Cameras › Camera and Aim.

Camera

You can also add a basic camera using the Add Camera to Grid icon

To select a camera to view you can use the panels drop-down and select the appropriate camera. This dialogue also allows you to go back to the default camera views and create a new view.

While you can modify the camera into position in plan view you may well find it easier to use perspective view as it allows you adjust the height easily.

Once you have selected a view you can use any of the Camera tools located in the View panel to Track, Dolly, Zoom, etc. to tweak the view.

Camera view

Camera location   Eye point

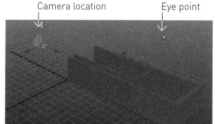

View →

Camera tools →

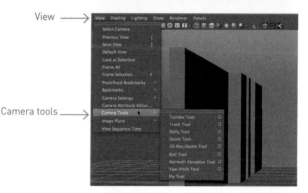

TEST RENDER

When you have the view set up you may well want to take a test render to see what it looks like.

Render view

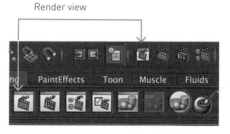

ADJUST COLOUR

If you need to adjust the material colour or tone you can select the object and open the Attribute Editor: Display › UI Elements › Attribute Editor. This contains all the attributes of the object, including the material and construction. You will be returning to it frequently.

Object Material Options

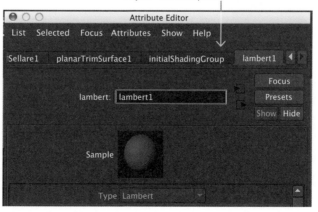

3: LIGHT AND BACKGROUND
ADD A LIGHT

The lighting options are available as an icon interface in the Rendering tab. You can add the lights in plan or perspective view and, once one has been added, you can copy it.

Point light option

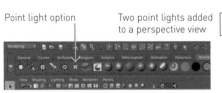

Two point lights added to a perspective view

Within the Lighting window panel you have the ability to use the lights rather than default lights and to check that shadows are on.

With a light selected you can use the Attribute Editor to alter the light intensity, colour, shadow type, etc.

Attributes editor

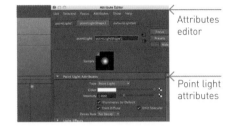

Point light attributes

ADD SUNLIGHT

You can add lights through the Lights icons or, if you have Mental Ray selected, you can add a default sky and sun to the scene.

Render Settings   Sun and sky

Test render with lights added

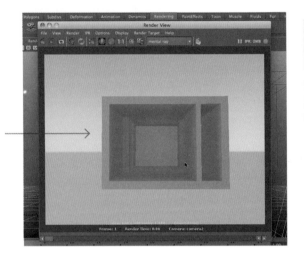

ADD A BACKGROUND IMAGE

When you add an image to the viewport it is also used in the final render environment.

You can import the image through the View panel

Rendered image with background

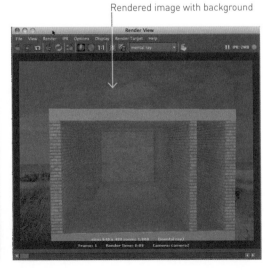

4: MATERIALS

The typical environment for creating a material would be Hypershade and the method of mapping a texture would be the Texture Editor. These interfaces can be very difficult to master but it's worth experimenting with them and enjoying their functionality.

Drag and drop materials from the Hypershade to object using the middle mouse button.

Go to Windows › Rendering Editor › Hypershade.

Place texture/image file/blinn material. Use middle mouse button to connect elements

A typical Hypershade interface showing materials and textures linked

UV Texture Editor →

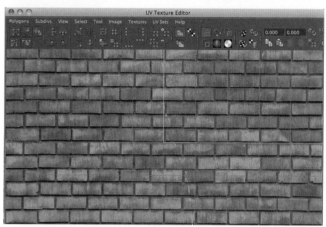

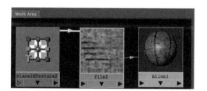

A simpler approach to adding texture maps to objects is to use the Attribute Editor. This was introduced earlier as a way of changing the colour and tone of a material, but you can also use it to add a texture/image map.

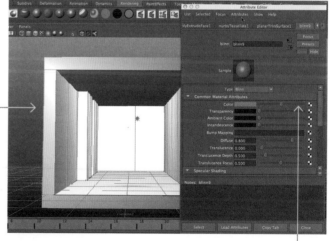

The object is selected

By selecting the checker icon a map can be loaded in the colour slot

A pop-up Create Render Node option will appear and you will need to select the File option. Once the File option is selected the Attribute Editor will give you the option to load the image file.

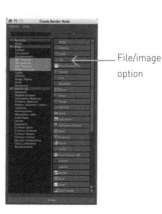

File/image option

As soon as the texture is loaded you will see it in the camera view as long as you have the Show Material in Viewport option selected.

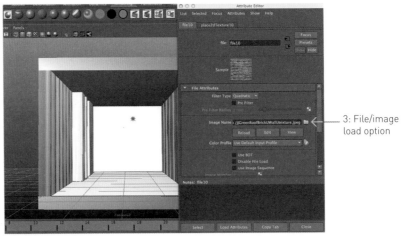

3: File/image load option

Show Material in Viewport

TEXTURING

Texturing is embedded within the Polygons tab menu not the Render menu. You can also access texture tools from the UV Texture Editor. The simplest way to texture/tile an object such as the wall of a shop is to use the Automatic Projection option as it does most of the difficult work for you.

Polygon tab   Automatic Projection texturing

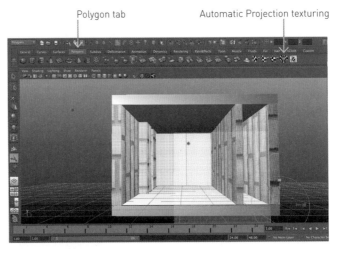

Automatic projection texturing Gizmo

You can also alter the scale of the texture map in 2D Texture Attributes.

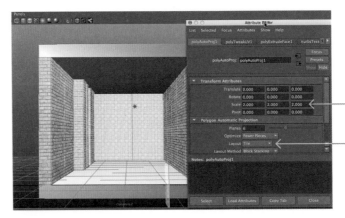

The scale of the initial map setting are incorrect but there are only a few options to change in the Attribute Editor, the scale and the type of mapping to tile.

Scale set to 2

Tile option

5: FINAL RENDER SETTINGS

We set the render settings at the beginning to Mental Ray so we now have the option of tweaking the GI settings. The image size can also be increased to produce a higher-quality render.

Common tab

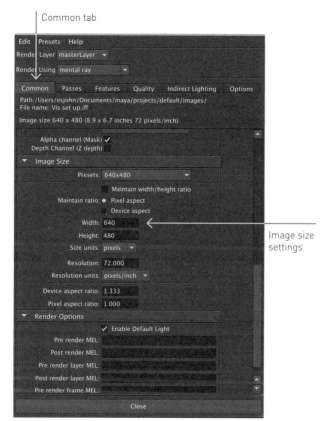

Image size settings

Indirect Lighting Tab

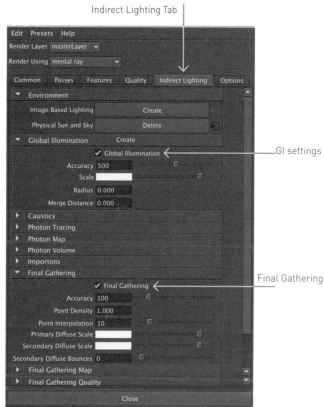

GI settings

Final Gathering

A final render view. File > Save Image and choose a format – tiff, jpeg, etc.

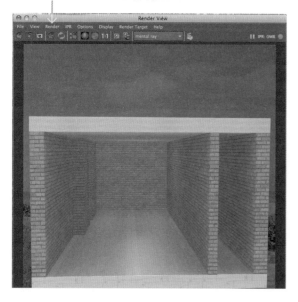

SketchUp rendering

1 : INTERFACE

SketchUp has evolved in many aspects of its object creation, but in terms of a default render engine it has not. The program does have shadow capabilities and does have a default sunlight setting that is used to evoke shadows in the scene. Normally in render programs you will process the image; this default in SketchUp is not possible. What you see is what you get as a final image. You can of course increase the image resolution to be of higher quality.

This may well be missing the point of the SketchUp program as it is essentially a sketching program, associated with measured hand-drawn activity rather than aspiring to the artificial environment often produced by CAD programs. It is with this sketch environment that SketchUp has developed myriad different sketch styles and effects that can be applied to a CAD model.

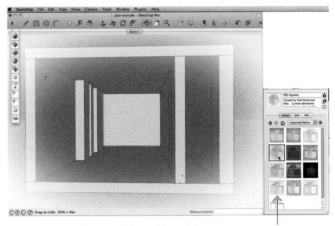

A typical sketch effect applied to a 3D model, with default shadows applied to the scene

Material sketch styles

Window › Styles for sketch rendering options

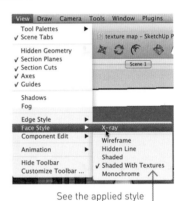

See the applied style

RENDER PLUG-INS

It would be a very incomplete explanation of SketchUp's rendering capabilities if we were to end the conversation there. In response and in partnership with SketchUp the render plug-in has evolved to give SketchUp enviable render engine capabilities. In line with the program's intuitive, simple setup, these plug-ins are very simple to use and the results can be nothing short of amazing.

Twilight, SU Podium and V-Ray are possibly the most common plug-ins available, although there are quite a few others on the market too. As a general rule they are purchased as an add-on and do cost! As with most programs for use in an educational environment, staff and student discounts are available. For the following example I have used the demo version.

I have chosen to use the V-Ray plug-in, as this is possibly the most widely used rendering program available. There are versions also available for 3ds Max, Maya and many other programs. So the information included here may well also be useful for using the plug-in in an alternative CAD program.

After the V-Ray plug-in has been installed it can be selected from the Tool Palettes windows menu. Window › Tool Palettes › V-Ray for SketchUp

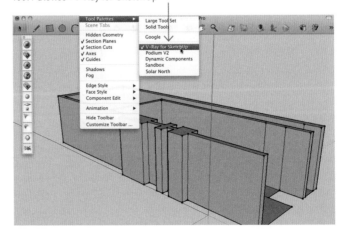

2: CAMERA

You can use the Position Camera tool to set up a camera view. This is available in the Large Tool Set or by selecting Camera › Position Camera.

As with other programs you select the eye point and the direction you wish to look in. You can set the eye height retrospectively or while using the measurements field.

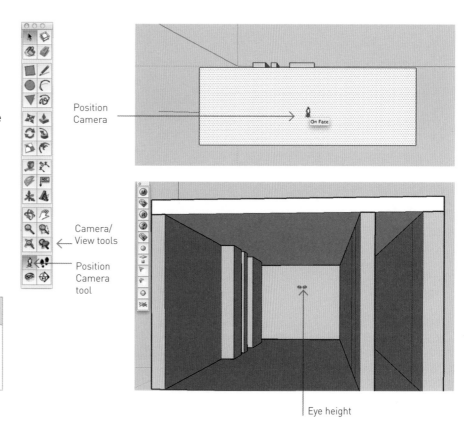

Position Camera

Camera/ View tools

Position Camera tool

Eye height

TIP EYE HEIGHT

When you use the Position Camera tool you can set the eye height in the numeric input box.

SAVING A CAMERA VIEW

Once you have created the view you will want to save it as a fixed view. You can use the standard views to navigate freely around the model. With the scene saved you will always be able to return to it:

Windows › Scenes

To save a scene you simply use the plus sign. The scene style is also saved with the scene.

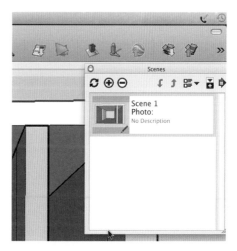

TEST RENDER

After saving a view you will probably want to do a test render. When you install and select the V-Ray render plug-in you will have an additional V-Ray tool set.

I have produced an impressive test render with no lights and simple white and pastel materials without having to alter any settings.

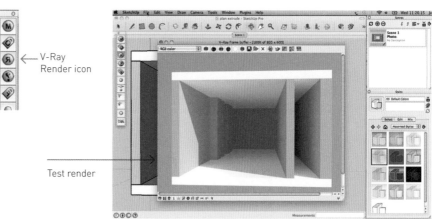

V-Ray Render icon

Test render

3: LIGHTS AND BACKGROUND

There are no lights except the sunlight in the native SketchUp interface, which is quite surprising. V-Ray and most of the other render plug-ins provide you with the ability to add spot lights, point lights, etc.

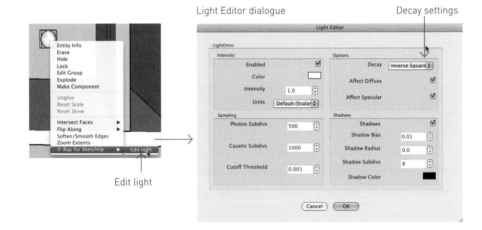

SketchUp's sunlight Shadow Settings
Window › Shadow

V-Ray point light

You can edit the light parameters by right-clicking on the light object and selecting Edit Light. You may need to change the setting from inverse square to linear.

Light Editor dialogue

Decay settings

Edit light

Colour Picker

TURN IT WHITE

After adding your lights you may want to standardize the materials to white. You can do this using the Colour Picker tool in the Materials palette.

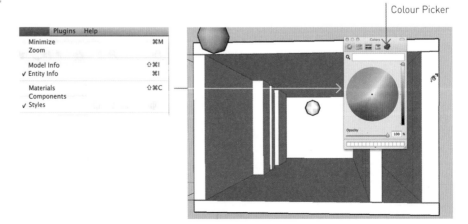

TEST RENDER

Here is a test render with the lights and materials both set to white.

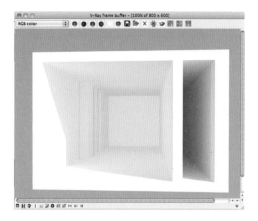

BACKGROUND

There are a couple of ways that you can use an image as a background, including by using the Match Photo tool. The easiest way to add an image to the environment is to select File › Import an Image.

The image will come in as a single image on a plane. You can then stretch and modify the image to an appropriate scale.

Imported image

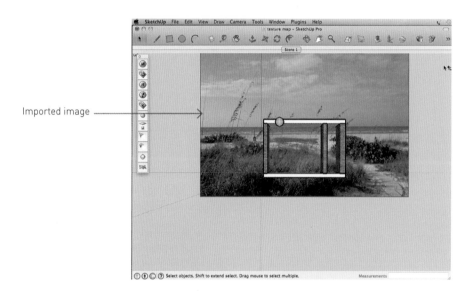

You can use axo view to help you place the image background

You can also use the Scenes palette to save additional views such as axo; this will ease the modification of the image plane.

TIP IMAGE IMPORT

This method of image background import is preferable to using the Material Texture option, as that will automatically tile the image.

4: MATERIALS

The Materials palette was introduced earlier (in the Turn it White section on page 146). There are lots of different predefined materials in SketchUp. To create textures you will need to select the Textures tab and make a new list. Go to Window › Materials.

When you create a texture you will be presented with a height and width dialogue; use this to scale the image map.

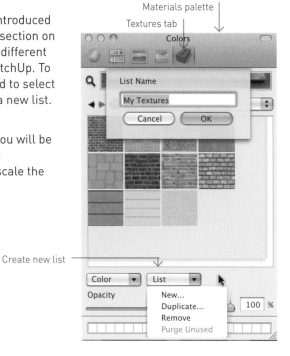

Materials palette

Textures tab

Create new list

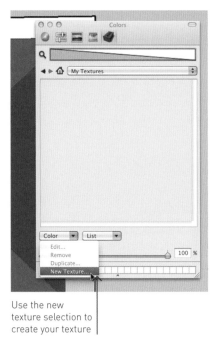

Use the new texture selection to create your texture

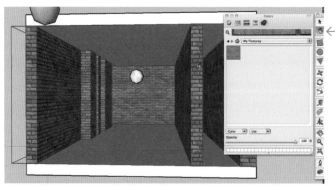

Once the texture has been created you can use the Paint Bucket tool to assign the texture

Test render with a material added

TEXTURE MAPPING

Texture mapping in SketchUp is quite a simple process. You can right-click on a face and use the Texture › Position tool to adjust the mapping, scale, position, etc. of the texture.

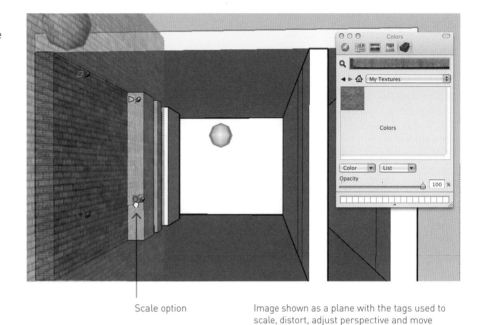

Scale option

Image shown as a plane with the tags used to scale, distort, adjust perspective and move

5: FINAL RENDER SETTINGS

You will want to make sure most of the settings in V-Ray are left alone; when you tinker with them it can drastically increase the render times. Check that the GI settings are on.

You can set a custom size in the Output settings

A V-Ray/SketchUp final render

Save image file

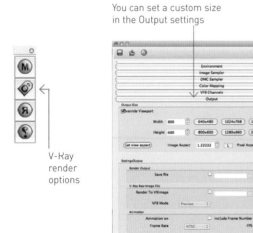

V-Ray render options

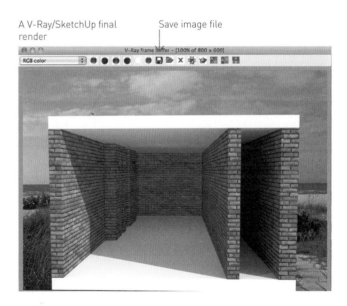

TIP GROUPING

Group an object to apply a material to the entire object.

FILE SAVE

Use the floppy disk icon to save the rendered image. To save a screen image, go to View › Export › 2D Graphic.

Vectorworks rendering

1: INTERFACE

Vectorworks has a unique interface for rendering – the rendering takes place within the program window. The render plug-in/program is called Renderworks and comes as part of the Vectorworks bundle. Overall, rendering is an intuitive and simple process.

You will need to familiarize yourself with the Palettes menu as you will most likely be returning to this frequently. From the Palettes menu you can open:

• The larger Tool Sets, which contain the visualization tool set.

• The Object Info palette, which contains many of the interfaces needed to visualize.

• The Resource Browser, which is the default way of creating backgrounds, materials, etc.

• The Visualization palette, which will allow you to select visualization elements in the scene, such as lights and cameras.

RENDER STYLES

There are many different render styles available, including many sketch styles. OpenGL is an interactive render that updates instantly and Renderworks Final is the highest standard of render.

To bring up the Custom Renderworks Options palette (right) go to View › Rendering › Custom Renderworks Options.

Palettes menu

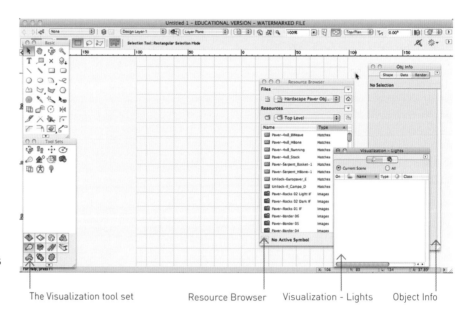

The Visualization tool set · Resource Browser · Visualization - Lights · Object Info

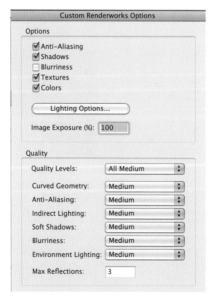

You can use the Custom Renderworks Options to increase the quality of your preview

TIP PALETTES

You may not want them all open at once! Toggle through them, use them when needed and close after use.

2: CAMERA

The Camera tool is located in the Visualization tool set. It is a simple place-and-point interface. Once placed, the Object Info palette holds all the tools needed to modify the camera, and also offers the ability to toggle between plan/top view and camera view.

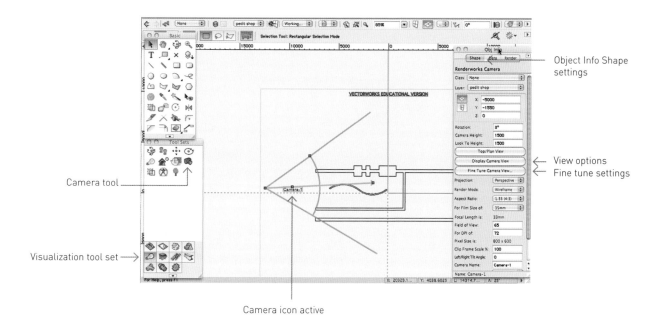

Object Info Shape settings

View options
Fine tune settings

Camera tool

Visualization tool set →

Camera icon active

FINE TUNE SETTINGS

The Fine Tune settings allow you to modify the view. Any modifications are saved. You will need to select the Fine Tune Camera View button to activate the tools.

Camera modify tools →

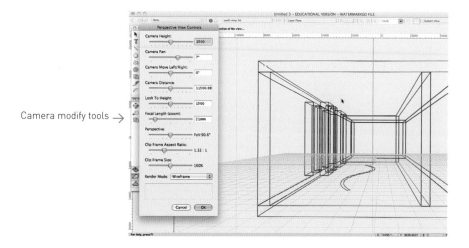

TIP FIT TO PAGE AREA

If you have set up a camera view and the view is distant rather than close up, use the Fit to Page Area command: View › Zoom › Fit to Page Area.

3: ADD LIGHT AND BACKGROUND

You can add a light by using the Light icon in the Visualization tool set.

After the light has been placed and selected you can set the type of light (point in this case) and the height of the light in the Object Info palette.

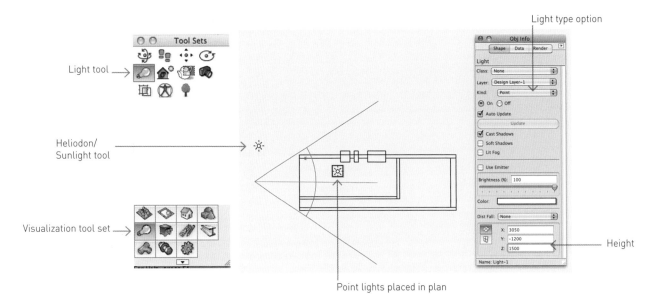

LIGHT EDIT

You can select any of the lights in the scene (and cameras) by using the Visualization palette. If you right-click on a selected light you can choose the Edit option.

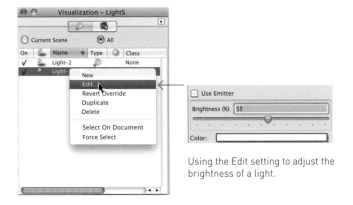

Using the Edit setting to adjust the brightness of a light.

SUNLIGHT

You can use the Heliodon tool to create natural sunlight for a scene. This tool allows you to set both the time and location of the sun.

BACKGROUND LIGHTING ENVIRONMENT

Vectorworks also has a multitude of set background environments that will add High Dynamic Range Lighting effects to a scene. HDRL can be used to create high detail in an image lighting setup be providing a larger tonal range. These are found in the View menu.

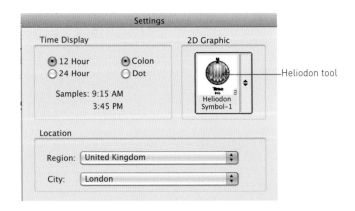

TURN WHITE/ADD BACKGROUND

The Resource Browser is a unique system of adding content to your scene. By right-clicking in the browser you will have the option to add an image as a background and to create a simple white material.

Once the resource has been created you can select it and use the right-click method to apply it to the scene.

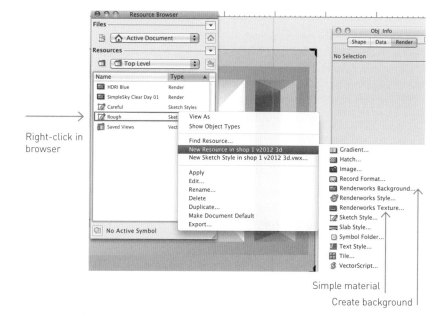

Right-click in browser

Simple material

Create background

Use the Apply option to assign the new resource.

NOTE: In the case of a simple white material you will have to select the object first before you apply the material.

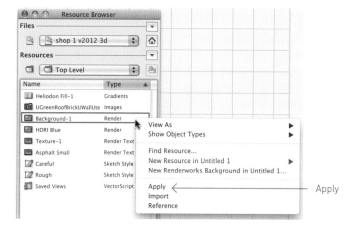

Apply

Test render with lights and background

4: MATERIALS AND TEXTURES

You create a texture by using the Renderworks Texture option. To add an image to a Renderworks material, use the Colour slot in the Edit Texture dialogue and select image.

You also have the option to add transparency, bump, etc.

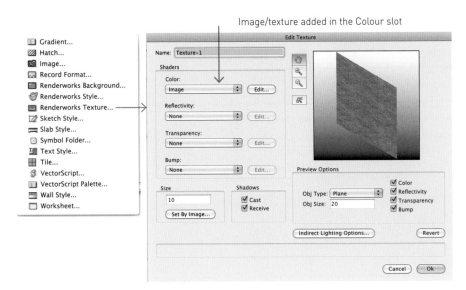

Image/texture added in the Colour slot

TEXTURE MAPPING

Once a texture has been created, select the object to texture and use the right-click apply method to assign the material.

You can use the Render tab in the Object Info dialogue to format the material.

The Scale option allows you to format the texture, effectively texture mapping the object. You can also alter the type of mapping required and even add decals.

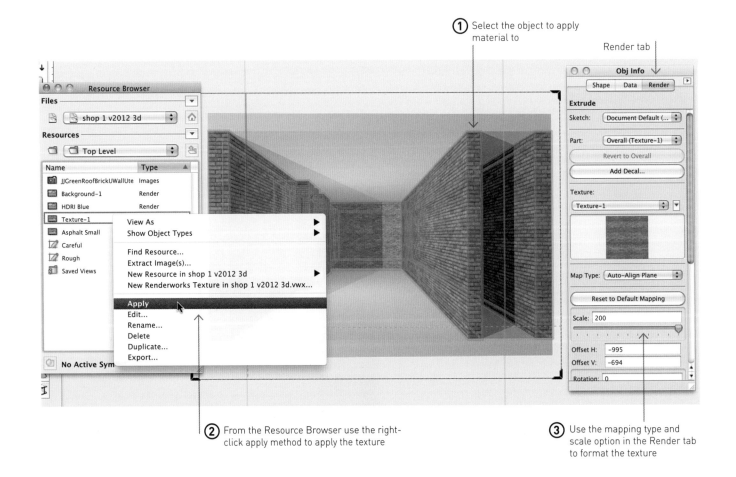

① Select the object to apply material to

② From the Resource Browser use the right-click apply method to apply the texture

③ Use the mapping type and scale option in the Render tab to format the texture

5: FINAL RENDER SETTINGS

You can now select View › Custom Renderworks Options to increase the quality of the render.

To produce a final render you can use the Batch Render function to create a high-res image. In the Batch Render settings you can set the image size and specify the output folder.

Go to View › Rendering ›Create Batch Render Job

Batch Render option palette

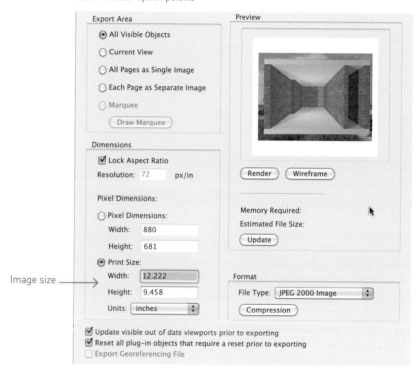

Your render will appear in the Available Jobs dialogue. You will need to transfer it to Chosen Jobs in order to process.

Start Batch Render

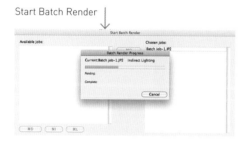

Image size →

TIP OUTPUT
Remember to specify the output, e.g. desktop.

TUTORIAL 3 RENDERING

This simple render exercise will introduce the fundamental methods for the creation of a polished interior perspective. A similar approach can also be used for exterior architectural perspectives: external renders tends to be easier to work with than interior.

When dealing with still imagery it is best to set up the camera/perspective view and develop the lighting, materials and context within this view environment. You will of course want a more holistic approach to the lighting model and context if you are intending to animate or take multiple perspectives from the CAD model.

Remember that when you are happy with the composition to increase the resolution to a desirable level and also if needed increase the render quality. Overall the production method provides a failsafe way to create an architectural perspective that is efficient in render terms and pleasing in visual terms.

Set your camera to eye height for natural perspectives

1: ADD A CAMERA IN PLAN AND SET YOUR PERSPECTIVE VIEW

With most software it is initially just a matter of getting the camera into the scene. Quite often you can just roughly place the camera and use the camera tools such as Pan and Dolly to track around a model. This gives you the creative freedom to select a view and can offer you some wonderful opportunities. When you find a view that you like you can always save it as a camera view so that you can return to it.

The easiest method for adding a camera is in plan view. You can easily reference the cone of vision and the field of the view. You may also want to set the height parameters in elevation view.

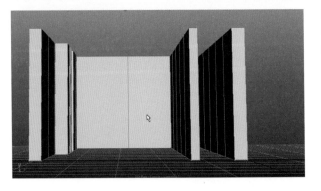

In this Maya example a camera is created in plan and moved into place.

The resulting perspective is not the desired view. Note: The view is set to Surface rather than Wireframe.

Using the various camera tools available, the perspective view is modified to become a better representation. As it is a camera view you can always return back to this set view.

STEP 2: TURN WHITE AND ADD LIGHTS

Less is more. Students will often add lights in the same way as you would encounter in real life, such as numerous spotlights. While in some cases this may be possible, it rarely gives you a good balanced image. It is best to balance the ambient lighting first and then possibly add accent lighting, such as spots and task lighting, afterwards. A better option in render terms would be to add spotlights in Photoshop.

To create a basic ambient lighting setup, use a sky light to add a natural feel to the scene; often with exterior views this may be the only light you will need. For interior views you should use one to three point lights to light the space. In both cases ensure that the shadows are initially on.

Using simple white materials and a simple lighting setup you will find that you are able to assess and develop the model perspective effectively in both interactive and final render modes. This is very important as it allows you to develop the perspective representation. For initial design proposals – for example, at the conceptual stage – this method of 3D visualization can be sufficient, if not actually preferable.

In this Form Z example, one sunlight and two simple point lights are used to light the scene. This type of setup is applicable to all types of software. The material of the shell has also been set to white.

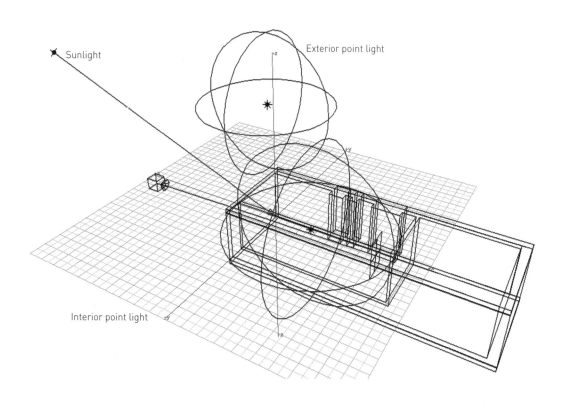

Sunlight

Exterior point light

Interior point light

3: ADD MATERIALS

If you have developed an effective lighting setup then a true reality in visualization will now depend on an effective use of materials. It's important to try out different materials in a scene rather than just accept what you think will work. While you will want to realistically describe the materials you are using in a scheme visual, you may find that if they are poor representations of that material then they will equally look poor in your visualization.

I have assigned these three textures to the model and they have been tiled (texture mapped) so they are in scale. The wood texture is a low-resolution image but works quite well when tiled and rendered.

Both the floor and ceiling textures have been applied to a surface object, rather than to the 3D form – both are effectively wallpaper textures. This can be a simpler method, since you only have to deal with a single face.

TWEAKING LIGHTS

The model setup is almost exactly the same as the basic one, but as the materials have different reflective properties I have increased the interior light source from 50 to 100 per cent. You will need to alter light levels after applying the materials.

Commonly referenced as textures, image maps are widely available on the Internet; you can get many textures that can be tiled so they become seamless. In creative terms it can be good practice to create your own textures. If you can match the scale and proportion of a material such as a wooden floor (with a little help from Photoshop) you can avoid having to tile a material.

TEXTURE MAPPING

Ideally the texture will go into the model at scale, but more often than not it will need tiling/formatting so that it fits the model.

TWEAKING THE VIEW

This view has exactly the same setup as the previous one. Here, though, I have tracked into the interior and tweaked some of the angles and foreshortening of the perspective. As an interior view it reads better than the model shell.

> **TIP** RESOLUTION
>
> While you need to have a good level of detail in any image that you are using as a texture, it is important the resolution of the image is not too high because this will significantly increase the rendering times. A suitable image size for a texture is 5 megapixels (500k). If your digital camera produces an output resolution any higher than this, you should reduce the image size.

4: ADD CONTEXT/SET THE SCENE

BACKGROUND

In both interior and exterior cases it is useful to add a background image. The image sets the environment and context. With an exterior view it will help create a level of realism by representing sky, ground and even surrounding buildings. For an interior representation it can add an interesting level of environment to reflective surfaces and a view out of the window.

It can take some time to find the ideal background image. Apart from trying to match a perspective view you will also need to set the mood.

I have booleaned an opening in the shop shell and added a simple beach.

Make some openings in the shell and try out different backgrounds and objects.

CONTEXT

Cars, chairs, tables and coffee cups all add a sense of living and reality to a model. While quite a bit can be done in Photoshop to contextualize an image it can sometimes be a painful process getting the correct angle of perspective. The added chair in this scene is one such example.

5: ADD AN URBAN CONTEXT

The shop model has been developed into a larger building and has been sited in an urban context. The image is taken from a Google Earth Street View – an extremely useful tool when searching for a suitable or actual context.

An underlay image is used to set the correct perspective view; this allows you to alter the view in Wireframe mode. The underlay is also used as a background for the final render.

The perspective of the building is matched to the view. This method gives you a quick and easy draft context that can then be worked up in Photoshop.

Image from Google Earth

Underlay to set perspective

Building sited with correct perspective

PART 4 PRESENTATION

INTRODUCTION

Analogue

In the days of hand drawing practice we would spend many hours redrawing (inking up) plans and sections for a final presentation. Many hours would be spent applying Transtext, a self-adhesive clear film for transferring title blocks and text, to annotate those drawings. From personal reflection I remember numerous perspectives being overcooked with a pencil render and having to redo the whole thing. As for contextualization, I often left that bit out, since the people I created in section often looked quite comical! Once we had spent the many hours needed to create our final drawings we would then often spray-mount them onto card for presentation. All this took time – a lot of time – and this was inevitably when you had an important deadline to meet.

Digital

Photoshop is universally the most important addition of all to interior and architectural presentation. It provides an unsurpassed fluidity in the production of layout, post-process rendering and contextualization. There are so many elements you can exploit within the program, but often you actually only need a limited tool set. The chances are you will have already used the program and so will be familiar with its basic functions.

Above
An example of a hand-drawn sheet with Transtext applied.

Below
An example of a simple Photoshop composite sheet.

Software

Unfortunately, of all the programs covered in this book, Photoshop is the only one that is not offered for free. There are student licences available at a discounted price, though, and you can always run a 30-day trial to complete a task. A free alternative to Photoshop (it has the same type of tool base) is the open source program called GIMP. The current version of Photoshop available is CS5; all the tools and methodology covered here, though, are just as relevant to earlier Photoshop editions.

Photoshop is now incorporated as part of the Adobe Creative Suite; this also contains other useful programs for the designer architect. Illustrator is a wonderful vector-based drawing program that deals well with architectural linework. Illustrator interestingly has a DWG function. InDesign is a layout program similar to QuarkXPress; when used for architectural layout purposes it can be an efficient alternative to excessively large Photoshop files.

While Photoshop is the king of programs, it is only as good as the user's intent. Its brushes, paint effects, text and visual ability are all useful tools, but what Photoshop cannot do is provide you with the creative solution. That is very much down to your use of the tools and your visual, artistic judgement. Luckily you can build on your skills in this area via the simple practice of sketching, using media such as charcoal, graphite, paint on a brush, etc. With the development of these core skills you will then truly be able to use Photoshop to its full potential. Without the key analogue skills you may well find yourself expecting miracles.

Above left and right
The work of Kobas Laksa reveals the extremes of what is possible with Photoshop annotation. In the Afterlife of Building series many prominent 'new architectural' structures (such as that on the left) were developed to become extremely realistic futuristic interpretations (right). The photomontages intelligently express the contradictions of contemporary urban development. The use of Photoshop is painstakingly realistic with many levels of detail and visual judgment helping to provide a convincing if not disturbing future view.

SETTING UP PHOTOSHOP

The first thing to consider when setting up a composite sheet is what paper size you intend to use. In Photoshop you can use the custom size option to do that.

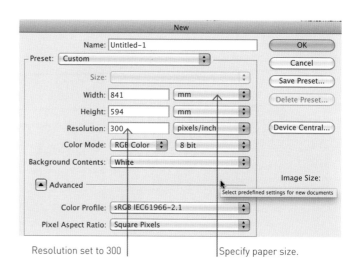

Resolution set to 300 | Specify paper size.

USEFUL PAPER SIZES

Size	Height x width (mm)	Height x width (in)
4A0	2378 x 1682 mm	93.6 x 66.2 in
2A0	1682 x 1189 mm	66.2 x 46.8 in
A0	1189 x 841 mm	46.8 x 33.1 in
A1	841 x 594 mm	33.1 x 23.4 in
A2	594 x 420 mm	23.4 x 16.5 in
A3	420 x 297 mm	16.5 x 11.7 in
A4	297 x 210 mm	11.7 x 8.3 in

The Interface

The Tool palette contains all the tools need to draw and paint. The Windows menu offers you the chance to make automated adjustments. While using Photoshop you will get to know the The Layers palette very well. While there is much functionality in Photoshop, we only need a limited tool set to achieve results

Open a pdf plan

Go to File › Open and navigate to the pdf file you require. Photoshop will automatically recognize the pdf file format.

The paper size will automatically be the page size set when the document was created.

The resolution MUST be set to the same size resolution that you set up in your new document or it will not come into the new document at scale. For example, if a plan is set to 150 dpi and then copied into a 300 dpi document it will be half its intended size.

Once you have opened your file Cmd + A (mac)/Ctl + A (pc) will select the plan. Cmd/Ctl + C will copy the plan.

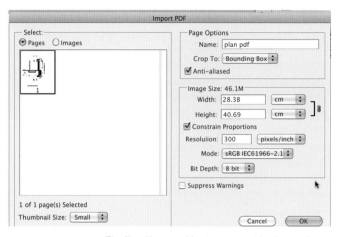

The file will open with a transparent background which is useful in underlay terms. The page size will be cropped to the limits of the drawing.

Select/Copy/Paste/Cut

Photoshop gets its speed and efficiency from being able to quickly cut, copy and paste from file to file or within a file. When you paste a plan or any item into a new file it will add a new layer. If you have selected and copied the plan you can go to your new file and paste it into the page using the keystroke Cmd/Ctl +] V.

Select and Modify

You can move the plan with the Select tool. If you want to rotate or apply a transformation to the plan/image then you can use the Transform tool.

Right click on the object and you can apply any of the Transform actions to it. Often in Plans and images there are areas that you will want to cut out. Use the Rectangular Marquee tool to specify the area and apply the Cut command to the drawing layer.

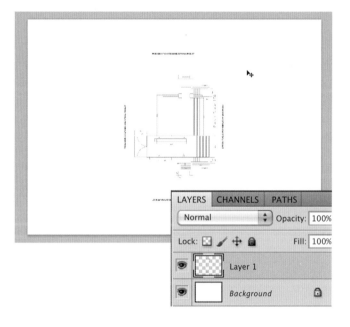

Image import

You can follow exactly the same principles of the plan import for images. In both cases you can actually miss a lot of the moves out and simply drag and drop the image or the plan directly into the file.

Layers

When you add an image using drag and drop or copy and paste, you will automatically create a new layer. When you have lots of layers it can be problematic, as quite often you will not be on the correct one and unable to edit. A simple way that you can select a layer is to right click on the image or plan and select it.

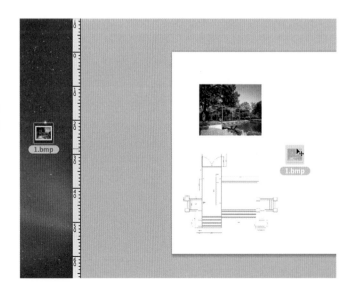

PRESENTATION POINTS

Cut and paste sheet

At its basic level Photoshop allows you to cut and paste a layout sheet. You can import a technical drawing to scale, bring in images and annotate with text. You can then save the file in a friendly format such as a PDF, then print, email or publish on the web. Within this composite sheet you can include all the content needed to sell or build your scheme.

Render fix

During the render process you will often find blemishes or areas of an image that you are unhappy with. Photoshop's tools gives you great flexibility for ironing out these faults. Sometimes textures will not behave the way you expect – a re-layering of the same textures in Photoshop is often a more efficient method for developing a visual. It can be better to develop a render with this in mind, knowing that faults can easily be rectified in Photoshop.

Below
A simple but elegant Photoshop layout with imported CAD plans.

Right
The background in this render has been replaced in Photoshop.

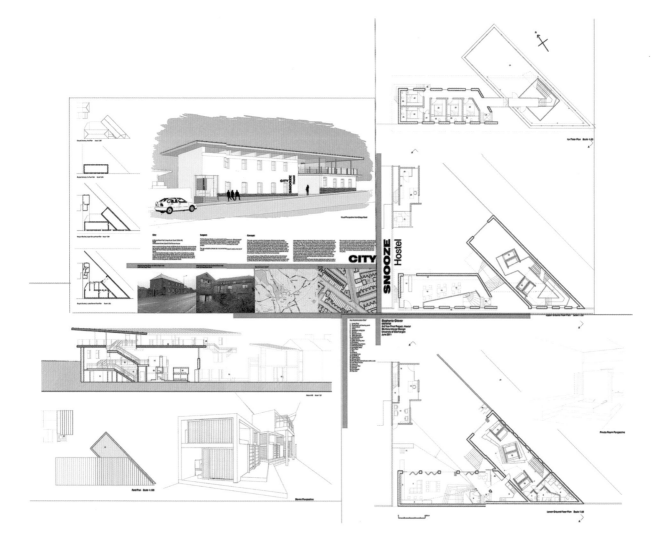

People

If people are added to a scene then visually this is the first place a viewer's eye connects with. It's human nature. A CAD model view of a human figure within a 3D scene will often undermine the entire image, as it can never match the integrity of a photographic representation. A far better approach is to replace this with a reference to human height and then Photoshop a photographic representation in. When adding people/objects to a scene make sure your selections are relevant to the context.

The eye line of the walking people is level

Above left and right
In this scene people have been added to create a busy setting around a restaurant.

Below
In this visual the directional light on the human figure helps to blend her into the scene.

Below
The impression of a tranquil, exclusive space is aided by the use of very few people in the scene.

Context

It is important to add references to an image to add to its contextual direction. You can write as many words as you like to describe the scheme but as the saying goes, a picture says a thousand words. Similar to the human instinct to look at the person first in the image, we also collate our understanding of what we are looking at by looking for day-to-day references, such as a computer, till or a table setting in a restaurant.

Light

As discussed in the rendering section, you can add lighting effects or the indication of lighting in a scene. However, too many lights can be a major issue in computation terms. While Photoshop does offer this functionality it's not a quick fix due to its 2D rather than 3D environment. But careful selection can effectively give the impression of lights in a scene, with the ability to add simple lighting effects such as lens flare.

Below
This street scene is a series of individual photos stitched together in Photoshop. Two youths and an older resident have been added to contextualize the image.

Bottom left and right
In this scene the light/lens flare and people have been added in Photoshop.

Tone and depth

In artistic terms computer-rendered images can appear clinical and uninviting. However, with the use of key Photoshop tools you can add a real sense of atmosphere and depth to a render by emphasizing the depth of tone in a image. You can create individuality rather than accepting a typical output. The Dodge and Burn tools provide this functionality.

Resolution

One primary rule with Photoshop, despite the ability to increase an image size, is that you will not be able to increase its quality any further than the original source. So in essence, if you have pixillated output then you can increase the file size as much as you like but it will still be pixillated.

There are filter options within Photoshop that allow you to liquefy pixels and in the right hands this can be a creative solution artistically. In architectural print terms you will need a minimum of 150–300 dpi resolution at print size to retain the line quality in technical drawings and the image quality of photographs.

Below
Three large-scale composite sheets: the visuals and arrangement were created in Photoshop.

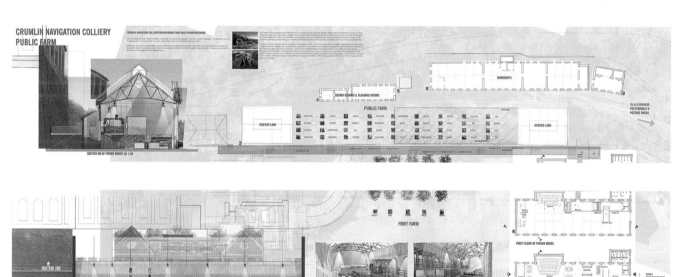

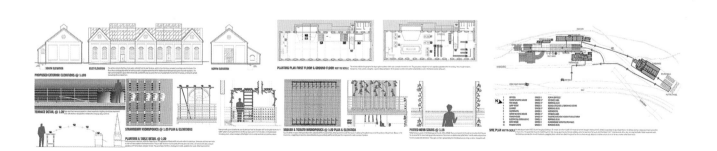

PHOTOSHOP TOOLS

ADDING TEXT

Text is added using the Text tool. You can click anywhere in the working window and type. Alternatively, you can click this tool and drag to create a text box.

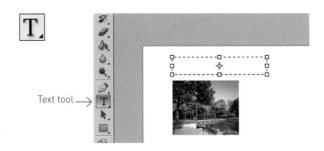

Text tool →

Note the three files opened while cut and pasting

Tool options

You can set the size, colour, etc. of the text using the tool options.

COLOUR

Colour can always be set for text and any object through the Set Colour tool icon.

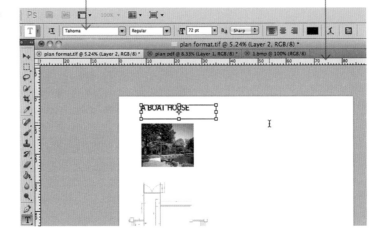

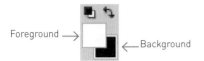

Foreground →   ← Background

LAYER OPTIONS

You can apply a layer style such as drop shadow to any layer present.

You can edit the text here. A double click will open the Layer Style palette

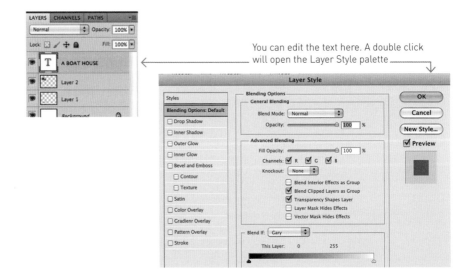

POST-TEXT FORMAT

Photoshop provides you with the typical character and paragraph formatting tools within the window palettes options.

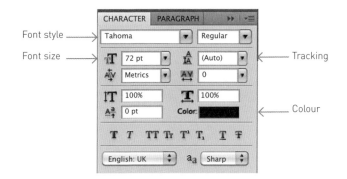

Font style

Font size

Tracking

Colour

PLANS FILLS AND OPACITY

Quite often in plan and section work you will want to annotate a material or surface, such as a facade detail or the tiling of a floor. Because the plan comes in on a transparent layer you can easily add colour, detail or pattern textures to the drawing.

Using Opacity often helps to soften any colour or image into the drawing.

Change percentage of opacity here

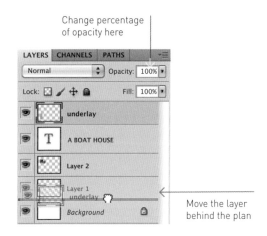

Move the layer behind the plan

Select an area to fill

Choose colour and use the Paint Bucket tool to apply. By choosing a 40 percent opacity we can still see the features of the plan.

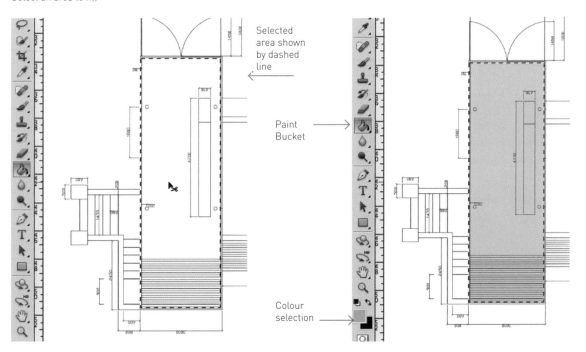

Selected area shown by dashed line

Paint Bucket

Colour selection

LINE TOOL

The Line tool can be found in the Shapes tool icon (if you right click on most of the icons you will bring up more options). If you have lots of linework then you may prefer to use Adobe Illustrator as it is a vector-based program more suited to this kind of work.

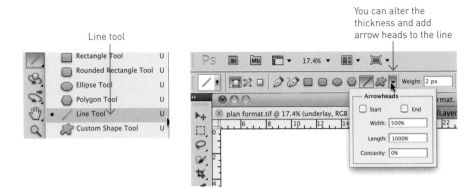

Line tool

You can alter the thickness and add arrow heads to the line

DEVELOPING AN IMAGE

Plan import and the set up of a composite sheet is a simple process. The next section deals with the tools that you use to develop a visual or photographic reference. The tools themselves are simple to use and increasingly interactive, showing you the results before you apply them.

As wonderful as the tools are, though, you will still need to judge what you do aesthetically, and that can often be the most difficult operation to master.

VARIATIONS

The Variations option allows you to preview different adjustments, such as darker and lighter. You can add colour variations to the image, which is often useful if you have an incorrect colour balance in an image. Variations allows you to apply multiple actions to the image. Go to Image › Adjustments › Variations.

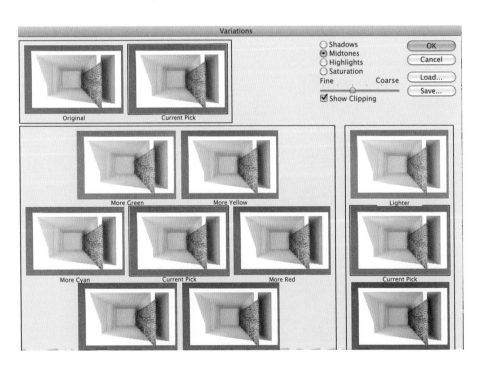

CURVES

Curves are a very effective way of adjusting the tone and exposure of an imported image. In many cases when the image is dark you can use Curves to expose hidden detail. Go to Image › Adjustments › Curves.

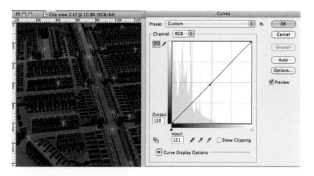

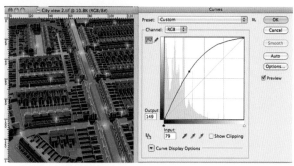

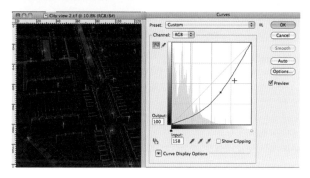

The original image with light to dark options

CLONE

This tool allows you to clone a selection of an image to another part. It's a wonderfully powerful tool for blending and adjusting image content.

It is important to first select the sample area with the Alt key and then define the distance you wish to offset the clone to.

In this example the Clone tool has been used to correct a rendering fault. It can sometimes be faster to clone a small area like this than to try and resolve in the render program.

Clone

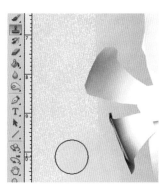

PATTERN STAMP TOOL

The Pattern Stamp tool is an offshoot of the Clone tool and lives in the same tool set (click on the Clone tool to activate it). You can create your own patterns and apply them to perform plan fills or texture an image render.

Pattern stamp

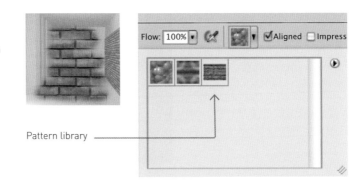

Pattern library

TIP SCALE

You cannot scale a pattern. You can either take a smaller or larger sample to get around this, or you can create the pattern on a different layer and use the Transform tool to scale it.

DODGE

The Dodge tool will lighten an image, adding tonal highlights.

Clone, Pattern, Dodge and Burn are all brush tools, so you can choose the size and type of brush you require. Within the options palette you can set the flow and also choose the All Layers option.

Dodge

Brush options   Flow/Opacity   All Layers option

Size and Hardness of brush

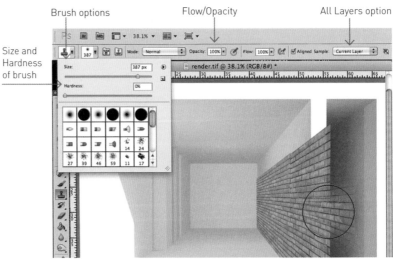

BURN

The Burn tool will darken the image adding tonal darkness.

Use the Pattern Stamp tool to apply a brick texture.

Burn

LIGHTS/RENDER

The Render option offers you the ability to add lights to an image. There are also many filter options within this menu. When the Lighting Effects option is used on an image you can select from multiple lighting options. The lighting effect is 2D, so may not always provide desirable outcomes, but with careful selection you can successfully apply a lighting effect to a specific part of an image. Go to Filter > Render > Lighting Effects.

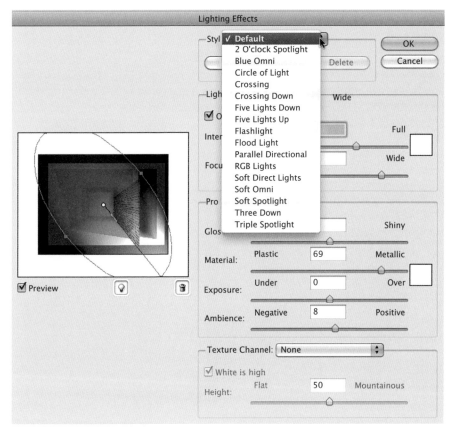

Lighting Effects options dialogue

LENS FLARE

When indicating light bulbs or lamps in a scene then Lens Flare is probably the best option. It will add a glow to an area rather than alter the entire image lighting. Go to Filter > Render > Lens Flare.

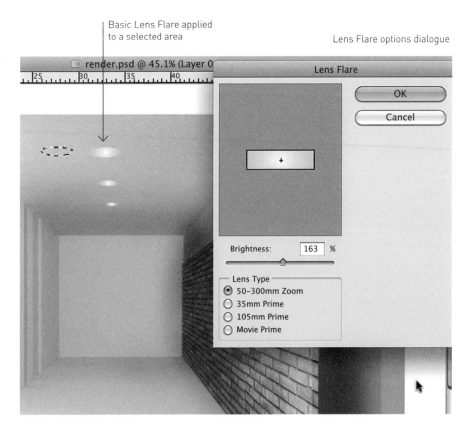

Basic Lens Flare applied to a selected area

Lens Flare options dialogue

TUTORIAL 4 PRESENTATION

This exercise is simple but contains all the elements you will need to post format a rendered view. Dependent on the complexity and render errors, you may find yourself dedicating far more time to develop a presentation image. It is true not only for Photoshop but for modelling and rendering that you can tell the difference between a representation that was created in 10 minutes and one that has had many days spent on it. The exercise introduces the process and relative tools; firstly to check, adjust the tonal range and to add textures and develop the depth of the image. Then we proceed to add lighting effects and people to the scene. Further annotation elements have been added to the scene such as pictures on the wall.

STEP 1

Start with a rendered scene. Open the image in Photoshop.

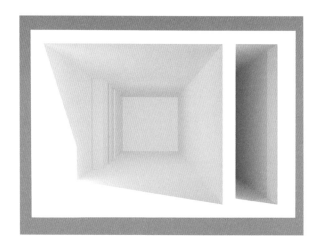

STEP 2

Use Curves to tonally format the scene, add more depth to the image or lighten.

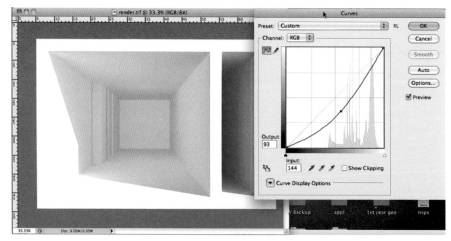

STEP 3

Drag and drop a texture or image into the scene.

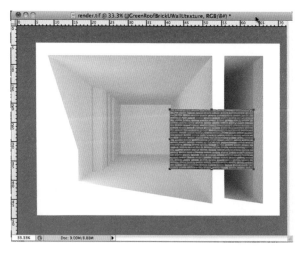

STEP 4

Use the Transform tool (Distort option) to place the texture in perspective.

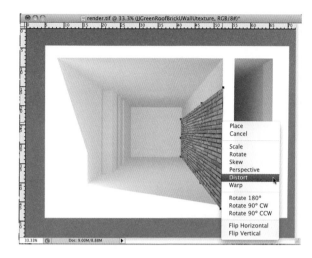

STEP 5

Copy and paste the texture image to create two versions. Use the Transform tool to scale and place them.

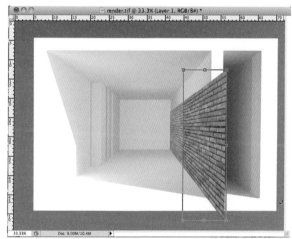

STEP 6

Use the Dodge and Burn tools to add more depth to the image. Use the Clone tool to iron out any seams.

TIP LAYERS

If you have more than one layer, then when creating the wall element use the Merge Layers option to unify them.

Use the right-click functionality to go between layers.

Burn

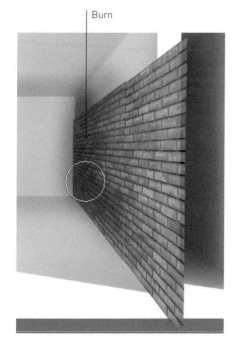

Dodge

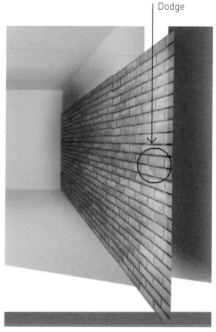

STEP 7

Use the Elliptical Marquee tool to select an area on the ceiling plane. Use the Lens Flare option to apply a lighting effect.

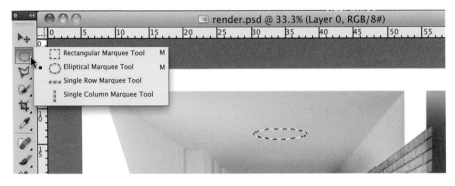

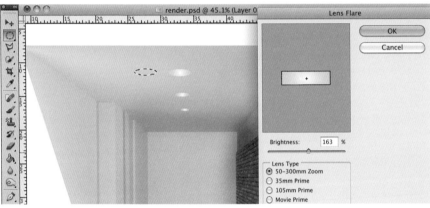

STEP 8

Add further textures to the scene and format as with the other textures. Use Distort and Opacity.

The ceiling plane has been extenuated by a simple copy and paste

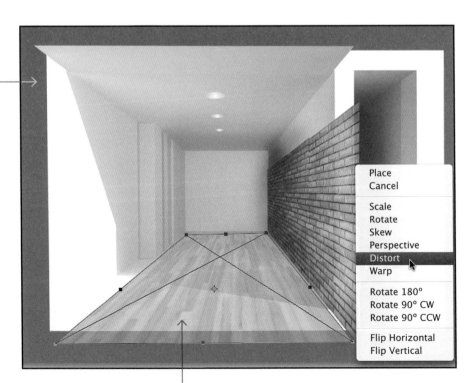

The floor texture has been added and distorted to fit the perspective

STEP 9

Finally, as mentioned already, it is often useful to introduce people to a scene, to add further context and provide a sense of scale.

The figures used in this perspective are on a transparent background, which means they can be dropped easily into the scene. Figures taken from photographs require a lot of work because you need to cut and trim away the background.

A small percentage of opacity has been added to blend the figures into the scene.

A hint of a human shadow has been added on a new layer, using the Brush tool

Eye line

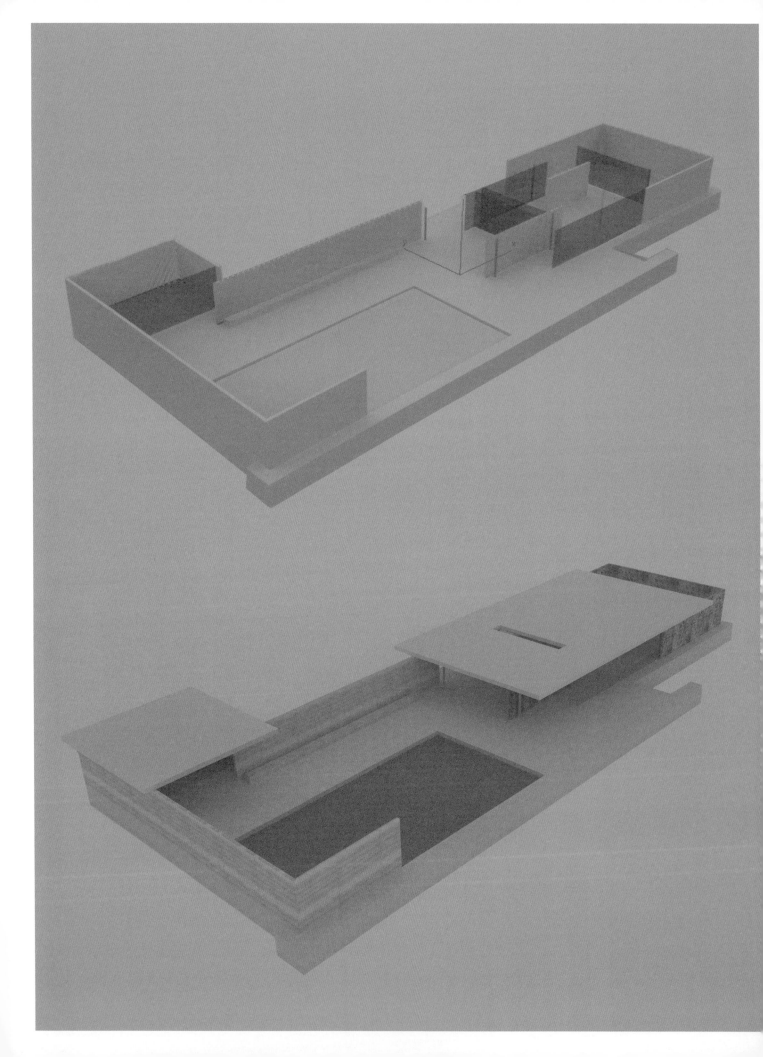

PART 5 OVERVIEW AND RESOURCES

FROM START TO FINISH: THE BARCELONA PAVILION

The following six pages bring together the drawing, modelling and presentation techniques that have been explained throughout the book. This is an overview of the CAD processes demonstrated in the previous four tutorials, using as an example the celebrated Barcelona Pavilion by Mies van der Rohe.

TIP LAYERS

You may want to put each section on a different layer so you can model them separately in 3D. When presspulling objects it is often useful to separate drawn elements using layers.

STEP 1

First draw the outline of the pavilion using the given dimensions. Draw the column details 180/40 and place them at the centre points indicated in the plan. Ensure that column details are placed centre to centre, as you would with measurements between columns.

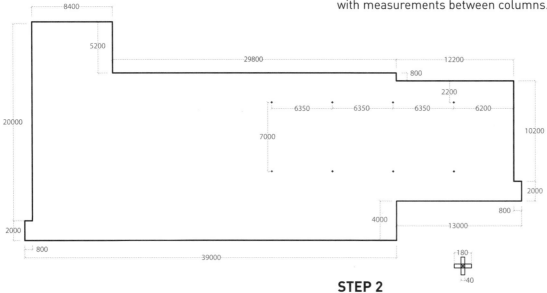

STEP 2

Draw in the external walls, pools and stairs using a combination of Lines and Offset. Tidy up any unwanted lines along the way using Trim or Delete. You may want to try the Array command for the stair detail or use Offset for parallel lines.

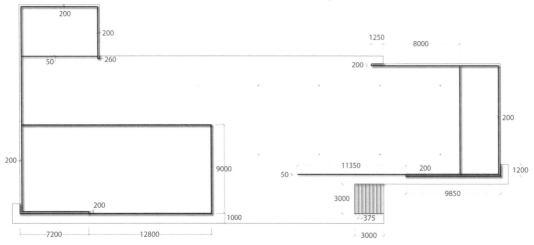

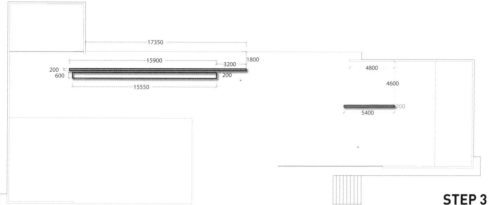

STEP 3

Draw in the lines to find the points in the plan [delete afterwards]. Proceed to draw the wall and bench elements. Use Offset to set up parallel lines and trim any unwanted lines.

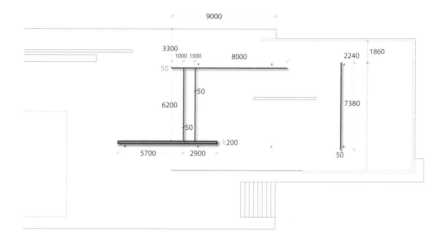

STEP 4

Draw in the lines to find the points in the plan [delete afterwards]. Proceed to draw the wall and glazed wall elements. Use Offset to set up parallel lines and trim any unwanted lines.

STEP 5

Finally draw in the lines to find the points in the plan [delete afterwards]. Draw in the two roof planes to the pavilion. Refer to the finished plan on the left for reference and to check that your plan is drawn correctly.

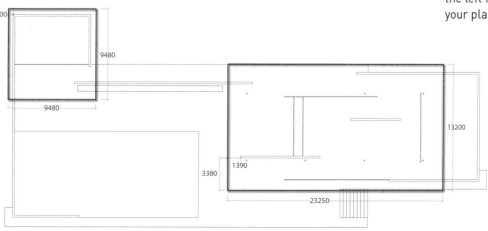

As the plan has been well prepared, the process of 3D construction should be simple. The building configuration (rectilinear) simplifies the construction. You may want to place the building floor plate on a different layer or redraw around the limits to create a closed object to extrude.

STEP 6

Place the plan in a 3D view such as ISO or Perspective. Presspull, extrude or box the floor of the pavilion using the height value of -1620 mm.

A negative value is used as it places the floor plate under the plan, so you will still be able to extrude the other elements.

STEP 7

Presspull, extrude or use the Option box to create the column details. Set the height value of 3000mm (note that all the objects extruded on the floor plate are 3000mm).

STEP 8

Using Presspull, subtract the pool elements at a height value of -1200mm. If you are unable to use Presspull, create a box the size of the pool and use Subtract to boolean the pool opening.

STEP 9

Add the stairs by creating boxes at 180mm increments, such as 180/360/540mm, etc. Again use the Subtract command to subtract from the floor plate.

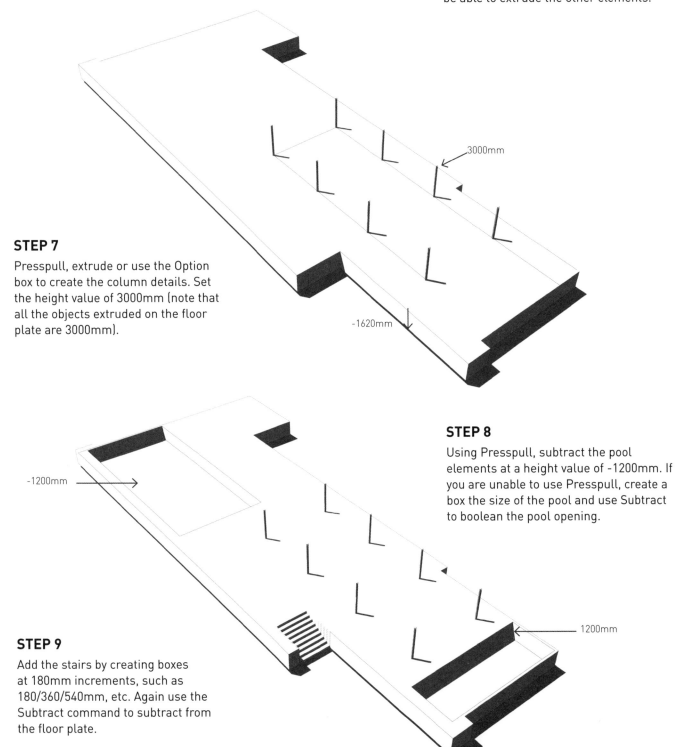

STEP 10

Create the wall elements by using a box command or Presspull. The height of all the wall elements is 3000mm. Use a height value of 450mm to create the bench element.

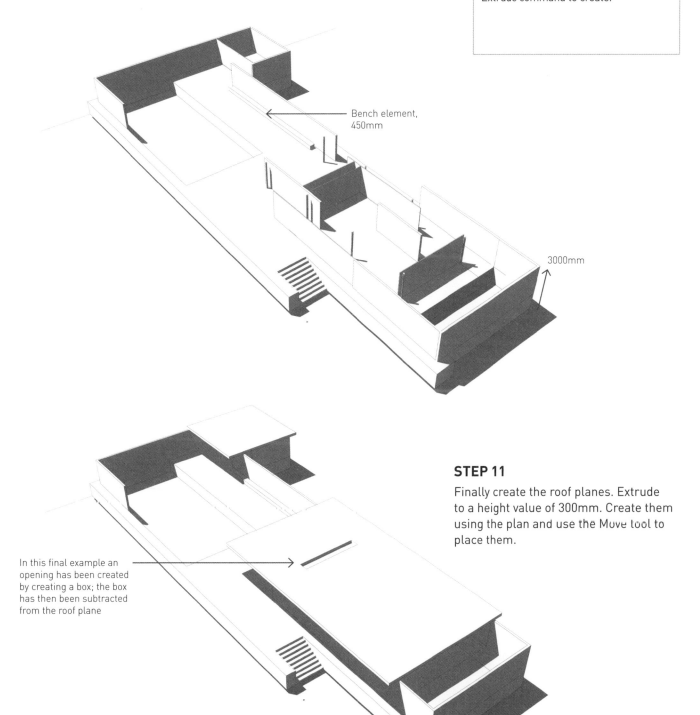

Bench element, 450mm

3000mm

In this final example an opening has been created by creating a box; the box has then been subtracted from the roof plane

STEP 11

Finally create the roof planes. Extrude to a height value of 300mm. Create them using the plan and use the Move tool to place them.

With simple lines and rich materials the pavilion lends itself well to visualization. With careful consideration given to textures and the environment it is possible to create a good computer representation. As always with computer rendering the resolution and render engine will play an important role in producing a reasonable image, along with some post editing.

TIP MATERIALS

You can create a new plane as a wallpaper if you want more than one texture on an object or you can select the face of a object and assign the material just to the selection.

STEP 12

Import the model into a rendering program. Here a plane has been added to give the model something to sit on, and cast shows have been added. Set the materials to white. Give transparency to glass walls and assign a chrome texture to columns.

STEP 13

Add a single skylight. Set the viewport view style to Realistic for a better visual representation. All the materials added are predefined and available with the render engine. Using Photoshop, you can create some of your own textures for marble walls, floor tiles, pool water, etc.

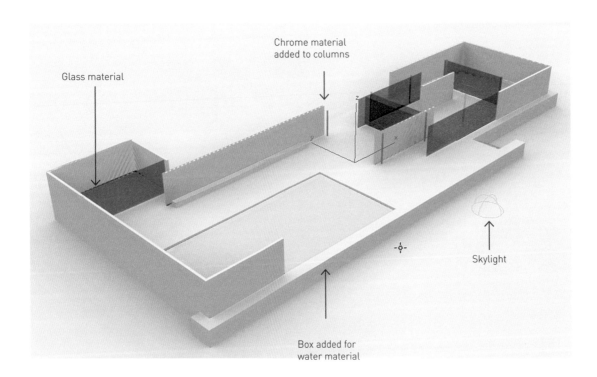

Chrome material added to columns

Glass material

Skylight

Box added for water material

The wall and the floor tiles are in proportion, e.g. the floor tile is equivalent to 1000 x1000 and the wall 3000mm x 3000mm. This makes life easier when texturing as you know the dimensions and proportions are going to be correct.

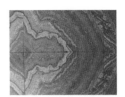

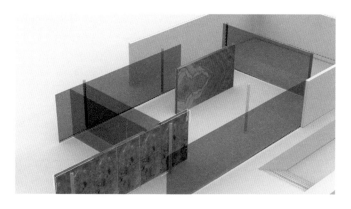

STEP 14

Assign the materials to the relevant walls and texture map them to ensure that they are tiled correctly. In this example there was no need to texture map as the onyx wall was prepared as a whole in Photoshop.

STEP 15

Add further details, such as a tiled pebble texture for the bottom of the pool, and ceramic floor tiles.

STEP 16

Checked that Final Gather/Indirect Illumination is activated. Tweak the material settings, adding specular and gloss to add some shine.

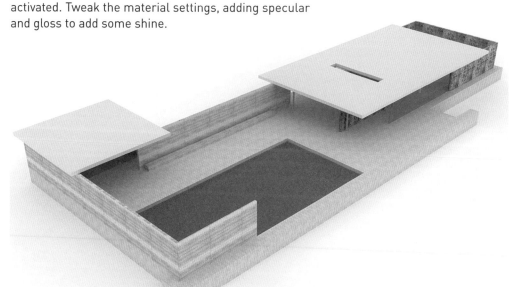

Initial test render with roof planes not hidden. A further texture is added to the entrance wall and is tiled six times

STEP 17

Add a camera to get a realistic view. Use a wireframe to set the model to an accurate perspective. Finally, add in a contextual background from a photograph, being sure to remove any distracting elements first.

BIM: BUILDING INFORMATION MODEL

BIM is an abbreviation of the term Building Information Model, and the concept is based on a single building model. The model contains all the design and quantitative information. Analytical tools are available to be used on the model, e.g. the cost of that specific model in square metres, the lifetime cost of the building, heat loss and gain predictions, bill of quantities and specification data, and so on. BIM allows us to test the physical reality of a building in a virtual environment.

It is a powerful concept: when you make a revision to the building model, such as window types, the model is able to re-cost the scheme. The model will also update and re-annotate any drawings automatically.

A BIM model is capable of combining design, quantity surveying, estimation, energy consumption, procurement, construction, operational cost and construction cost. While still in its early stages, and still prohibitively costly enough that it is not yet widespread within the industry, BIM will undoubtedly revolutionize the architectural industry in the same way CAD did in the 1990s.

BIM is often used as an architectural buzz word. There are many supporters of the concept who suggest that BIM could eventually replace many of the mainstream programs used in architectural CAD and production. On the down side, through the process of total automation it is possible that judgements may become based purely on cost and BIM buildings could become bland, functional objects. However, equally there is a positive outlook, and many believe that BIM offers the chance for a truly integrated and cost-efficient process of design and construction.

If the BIM model does come of age, it's important to note that there will still be plenty of demand for the ability to sketch and draw by hand and digitally.

BIM workflow

While there are variations in the way you can adopt the capabilities of BIM software, all programs share a typical method of working that can be applied to architectural practice. The 'single file model' is the most important aspect of the BIM concept.

- Create the site and a mass model of the architectural object.
- Divide that mass model into floors.
- Develop the external and internal structure, define ceiling planes and roof types.
- Add internal and external walls, doors, window openings, stairs.

The real-time nature of the components links all the design and quantitative data together; it can then be used to generate drawing sets, visuals, construction details, costings and construction schedules.

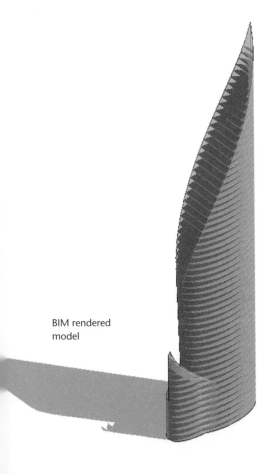

BIM rendered model

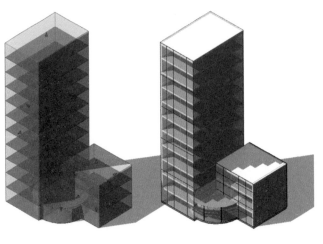

Mass model   Model with walls/floors/windows

Revit

Revit has been around for some years, purchased by Autodesk in 2002. Out of all BIM interfaces it has worked on developing the BIM concept as the core aspect of the program interface. It is indeed unlike 'normal' CAD software. It requires a sound understanding of the software concept as much as it does the ability to draw.

The power of the software comes from the ability for many professionals to work in tandem on a single building model; you may have one person developing a construction detail, while another would be looking at specifying the window type. Revit has an inbuilt 'Conflict Check' to ensure two people cannot alter the same element of the file at the same time.

REVIT INTERFACE

Ribbon with Massing and Object tools

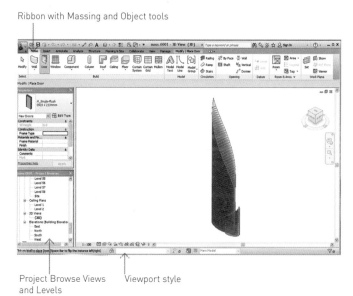

Project Browse Views and Levels　　Viewport style

From the model you can then create elevations, sections, perspectives, etc. On a basic level you can create renderings, but where Revit comes into its own is the ability to perform a conceptual energy analysis, energy performance analysis, structural analysis, solar analysis, etc. Change the window type or the insulation values and the data will be automatically updated.

On completion of the model it is possible to create schedules, quantities, and material take-offs to quantify and analyze the components and materials used in a project.

WORKFLOW

1) Create the project. Create site plan; define the building PAD; add additional information, roads, existing trees, etc.

2) Create a mass model. Create in place in the scene or import and place a mass object in the scene

In-Place Mass　　Place Mass

3) Add levels [define floor plates]

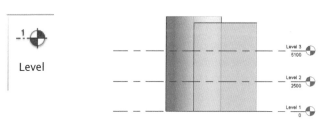

Level

4) Create floors, walls and roof from the mass model

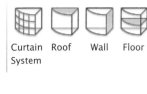

Curtain System　　Roof　　Wall　　Floor

5) Add structural columns and beams; add Internal and external walls, doors, windows openings; add roofs, floors, and ceilings; add stairs, partitions, rooms, components [furniture elements]

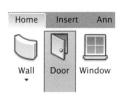

Wall　　Door　　Window

Use home tools to add detail to model

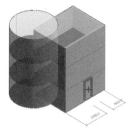

AutoCAD Architecture

While AutoCAD is not a BIM program, AutoCAD Architecture is – with the benefit that its interface is based on AutoCAD so you will find it familiar and can quickly get into your stride using the parametric BIM tools.

In terms of design and documentation it's a very useful program to run alongside AutoCAD. You can draw windows and walls that have real-world construction information, and generate real-time sections and elevations that update as changes are made to the model. It has an integrated render that is becoming more refined and developed. You can also create schedules that are directly linked to your design and perform area calculations.

WORKFLOW

You can start with mass objects and then define the floors, as you can in Revit, or use a basic floor plan, add walls and floor slabs, columns, etc.

AutoCAD Architecture can help you to automate the creation of walls, windows, openings, doors, curtain walls, and even adding stairs to a AutoCAD plan. Once complete you can then switch back to AutoCAD and carry on modelling and drawing.

Architectural design tools   Section tools

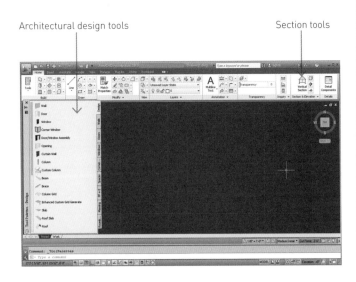

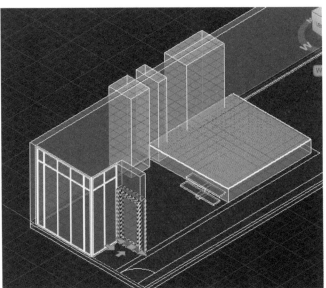

The shop plan from the tutorial is imported into AutoCAD architecture and the design tools used to add walls, windows, floors and stairs.

BIM TERMINOLOGY:

Project: the 'project' is the single database of information for your design'

Levels: roofs, floors and ceilings

Divisions: divisions segment the building in the horizontal plane

Constructs: A construct represents one unique portion of a building, such as a building core

Elements: an element is a generic building block for multiple use, equivalent to Blocks in AutoCAD

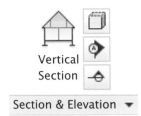

You can take a 3D model from AutoCAD and use the Section tool in AutoCAD Architecture to create sections and plans [though the very latest version of AutoCAD now has a section plane tool]

Vectorworks

Vectorworks has for some time contained elements associated with the BIM concept. The Tool Sets palette follows the typical BIM workflows you use in programs such as Revit. Site Planning and the Building Shell tool provide parametric building objects that interact with each other.

When using Vectorworks you will already be following a BIM type workflow, such as massing a building and deriving floors from the model. On a basic level, using the Building Shell tools allows automation when creating windows and doors. The MEP tools set Mechanical, Electrical and Plumbing. MEP allows you to create and design the map infrastructure to develop further the detail (and data) of the model. To further the workflow you are able to link the object to data specification and quantification.

Vectorworks BIM tools

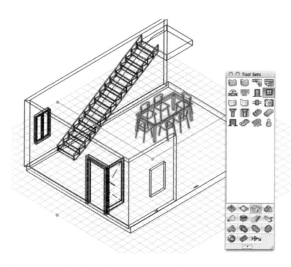

Vectorworks Building Shell tools; predefined stairs, furniture, windows and doors

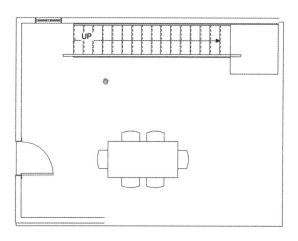

The same model in plan view with the correct annotation for the doors, windows and stairs.

Summary

In practice the Building Information Model should be the perfect development of CAD, a seamless integrated tool for designing, managing and constructing an architectural build. But with this concept there comes risk, the risk of things going wrong, incorrect human interaction with the software; computers by their very nature are temperamental, and that's putting it politely. If I can relate my own experience of corrupt files, of days of work lost when creating plans or trying to render a view and then the whole thing crashes, leaving me in a hopeless position and having to start the whole thing again. One has to question whether 'putting all your eggs in one basket' is a wise thing to do. That said, there are many elements and capabilities of the BIM concept that will undoubtedly transform CAD's relationship with building.

Troubleshooting tips

The following are some common problems that you may experience when using CAD software. The list is not extensive or software specific, as that may well take a book in itself, but it will help with some of the issues that you will most often encounter. It's a good idea to keep a small journal handy, to write down any problems and solutions that you come across; you can refer to this when needed, and even share the information with colleagues. With the proliferation of information on the internet, it's also usually possible to find a solution to any problem you encounter when using CAD software.

Working with computer-aided-design is by its very nature a problem-solving exercise and – as with most problems we are presented with – there may be many ways of reaching the same solution. If you don't succeed, then try another way. As a learning process it is like riding a bike, and once you resolve a problem you will always remember that solution. You will gain knowledge through experience and that can be rewarding, as there is a sense of achievement in building a skill base. As CAD computing is such a progressive medium it's refreshing to know that there is always someone who knows more than you around the corner, and it's the very fact that you learn something new every day that makes the subject so interesting.

Installation

Activation After you register and install software you may need to activate the software. You may need to register a new account during the activation process.

30-Day trials You can usually install a free 30-day trial; 30 days can often be enough time for you to complete the project you are working on.

Importing

Format If you open up a drawing and it's in the wrong measurement format, change the UNIT Type of a drawing.

DWG import 3D imports (particularly into SketchUp) can be problematic; often you will only import the 2D information. **Test any move between software before you commit.**

DWG import scale If a model imports and disappears, scale the drawing before import and work in a higher unit of measurement (eg metres rather than mm).

DWG import orientation The drawing imports on its side or way off the origin. If this happens, prior to import rotate and place the drawing on the 0,0,0 origin in your drawing software.

3D model import Model imports as a single object: use an Entity or check a Group option has been deselected in the imports dialogue to preserve the individual objects.

Import scale Often when you import a pre-built object, such as a chair, it may not be at the correct scale. Use the Scale option to resize it.

Display/Environment

Zoom You have 'lost' your drawing on screen: Zoom Extents will fit all the drawn information in the working window.

Line weights Make sure the Display Line Weights dialogue is ON, so you know what you are working with.

Dotted line Set the scale of the dotted line in the properties so you can see the dots.

XYZ Unable to draw on the default XY axis? Reset the XYZ to WORLD.

Slow machine Use Wireframe rather than Realistic Visual mode when working on a project.

Visibility If you create something and it's not showing, check it is visible or the layer options are set to visible.

User Interface If you lose any tools, reset the user interface to default.

Create and Modify

Command Unable to use a command? Use the Escape or Return key to exit a tool.

Keyboard entry problems Remove your hand from the mouse when entering any dimensions in a data/command field.

Command input Read the command line/tool info at all times, it will inform you of the next move or of your tool options.

Wonky lines Ensure the Ortho mode (or Shift) has been selected.

Gaps in linework Check your snaps are activated and you are snapping to the end of the preceding line.

Press pull isn't working Check for broken lines, and ensure there are no gaps.

Array Create a simple array and then use the Properties palette to format the array to your requirements.

Separate elements If your object will only move in bits, use the Group, Compound or Union option to make it a solid object.

Move Only able to move up or down? Check to see if Ortho or Parallel is activated.

Isolate/hide Use the Isolate/Hide option to work on individual objects.

Rendering

Flat Image No shadows are on.

Lights Are these not working? Check and alter the intensity/decay settings in the Light Edit properties.

Overexposed image Check the light values and reduce them if necessary.

Global illumination Use low light volumes and multiply with the Global illumination multiplier to gently and realistically increase light levels in a scene.

Textures Textures don't show up when assigned? Make sure that Show in the Viewport option is selected and UVW/texture map the object.

Poor resolution Ensure the resolution of the render is at a suitable size for print (usually 300dpi at the size it will be used on the page).

Slow render preview Reduce the image size and the other render settings to draft or lower.

Not enough RAM to render an image? Use the Region option to render a bit at a time.

Fuzzy image Increase antialiasing values if image becomes jagged or has fuzzy details.

Post process

Rendering faults Use the Clone tool to iron out any mistakes.

Incorrect layer Ensure you have the correct layer that you wish to alter activated.

Dull image Use image adjustments to add depth.

Montage Combine the best bits of various images to create a final image.

Increasing resolution There is no point increasing the resolution of an image in post process as it is set at the point of creation, ie during the render or photograph.

Software comparison chart

The following table provides a basic overview of each program's strengths and weaknesses. Almost all are available on either a free or time-trial/demo basis. You will find the compatibility section useful when planning ahead any transfer of a CAD file to another software type.

Software	PC	Mac OS	2D/3D Use	Free licence type	GI rendering	BIM capabilities	AutoCAD compatibility	Customize user interface
AutoCAD	YES	YES	2D/3D	Student/Academic free	YES	NO	good	YES
AutoCAD Architecture	YES	NO	2D/3D	Student /Academic free	YES	YES	good	NO
Vectorworks	YES	YES	2D/3D	Student/Academic free	YES	YES	good	NO
SketchUp	YES	YES	2D/3D	Academic cost or limited free version	NO [plugin option]	NO	poor [2D import ok, not 3D]	NO
3ds Max	YES	NO	3D with 2D tools	Student/Academic free	YES	NO	good	NO [previous version options]
Maya	YES	YES	3D with 2D tools	Student/Academic free	YES	NO	poor [scale issues]	NO
Form Z	YES	YES	3D with 2D tools	Student/Academic free	YES	YES	good	NO [previous version options]
Revit	YES	NO	3D with 2D tools	Student/Academic free	YES	YES	good	NO

Glossary

additive methods of construction
Creating 3D shapes by merging two existing shapes to form one volume.

analogue
The opposite of digital: in this case, the many drawing and modelling techniques requiring paper, pen, pencil, spray mount and tape that provide valuable preparation for the designer before entering the digital world.

AutoCAD Architecture
A version of **AutoCAD** designed to meet the specific needs of architects. Versions have existed since 1998.

AutoCAD
The CAD software package developed by Autodesk, first released in 1982, regularly updated, and still among the most popular today.

BIM
Building Information Model(ling). The creation of a digital model of the physical and functional characteristics of a proposed structure. An extended and specific application of CAD technology.

boolean modifiers
The Union and Subtract commands, or their equivalents, in a CAD package. Used in **additive** and **subtractive means of construction**.

Cartesian coordinates
The system used by CAD packages to describe points in three-dimensional space, consisting of three values describing the point's position along perpendicular axes labelled X, Y and Z relative to a fixed origin. Named after the mathematician René Descartes.

command line
A computer interface with which a user controls a program or operating system by inputting a series of text commands.

endpoint
The end of a line or object in AutoCAD. The cursor can be set to snap to these when drawing new objects, avoiding the need for construction lines.

external reference file
A file brought in as a separate layer for reference when creating a design, and then switched off when no longer required.

faces/facets
The two-dimensional shapes which make up a three-dimensional object.

instance
A duplicate of an object that remains linked and identical to its source.

isometric
The most common form of axonometric projection. A method of drawing a 3D object in which distances along each of the three axes are rendered to the same scale, with no sense of perspective.

JPEG
Joint Photographic Experts Group. A file format for displaying photographs and other digital images. JPEG files allow a variable rate of compression, with a consequently varying degree of quality.

layers
A method of organizing information within a CAD or other graphics program. Many properties of an object are overlaid within the same digital space, but can be switched on or off individually to be viewed or manipulated in different ways.

Maya
A 3D graphics program currently owned and developed by Autodesk. First produced by Alias Research in 1998, it is used primarily for animation, visual effects and video game design.

Mental Ray
A 3D-rendering application developed by Mental Images. It is available as a standalone program as well as being integrated into software including **Maya**, **3ds Max**, **AutoCAD**, **Revit** and **SolidWorks**.

mesh
Another way of describing a **facet** or **face**, referring to their similarity to a physical wire mesh.

modification
An operation that changes an object after it has been created, usually from a simple to a more complex one.

navigation
The features of a **user interface** concerned with moving between the various other features of the program itself.

orthographic
A representation of a three-dimensional object, including views from three perpendicular directions, such as from the front, top and side. It may also show rear and bottom views, etc.

parametric design
Design processes in which a shape is generated from initial parameters and mathematical functions.

PDF
Portable Document Format. A file format created by Adobe to display fixed-layout documents. Each PDF contains all the information required to display or print the document on any compatible device.

Photoshop
A graphics editing software package by Adobe, dating back to 1990. Primarily a **raster** editor, it has become the industry standard for graphic designers and photographers.

pixellation
The effect observed when zooming in on a **raster** image. Individual pixels become visible and the image reveals an unnatural, 'blocky' appearance.

plan export
Transferring a plan or design from one 3D program into another.

polygon object
A description of a three-dimensional object referring to its construction from individual **facets** or **faces**, each of which consists of a polygon.

presentation drawing
A representation of a design, annotated and rendered with appropriate lineweights so that it can be most clearly communicated to others.

raster
A raster-based image is constructed from a grid of minute pixels (picture elements). Also known as a bitmap or dot matrix.

Revit
The industry standard **BIM** software package, acquired by Autodesk in 2002 from Charles River Software, the startup who first released it in 1997.

SketchUp
An easy-to-use 3D modelling program developed by @Last Software, first released in 2000 and acquired by Google in 2006. It features access to an extensive online library of pre-designed objects, known as 3D Warehouse.

SolidWorks
CAD package that has been produced by the SolidWorks corporation since 1995.

subdivision
A method of increasing the number of **facets** of a three-dimensional object, by breaking up the existing facets, so that they may be edited individually.

subtractive methods of construction
Creating 3D shapes by removing or 'carving away' the space occupied by a smaller shape from a larger one.

surface object
A collection of lines that form a closed two-dimensional object.

3ds Max
A 3D graphics software program currently developed by Autodesk and aimed at artists and animators. An alternative version, 3ds Max Design, includes features aimed at architects, designers and engineers for visualizing projects. Formerly known as 3D Studio Max and first produced by the Yost Group in 1996.

user interface
The means by which a user interacts with a specific piece of hardware or software, encompassing all the tools available, their function, layout and appearance.

vector
A vector-based image is constructed from geometric objects such as lines, points, curves and shapes. Vector images can be enlarged without any **pixellation**.

Vectorworks
A CAD and **BIM** software package produced by Nemetschek Vectorworks. Originally known as MiniCAD when first launched in 1985.

V-Ray
A 3D-rendering engine produced by Chaos Group since 2002, available as an extension for a number of CAD and graphics packages, including **SketchUp**, **Maya** and **3ds Max**. Used by film and video game designers as well as architects to make realistic visualizations.

wireframe
A simple representation of a 3D object in which only its edges and vertices, along with lines along its curved surfaces, are shown.

XYZ
The **Cartesian coordinate** system used by CAD packages, consisting of three perpendicular axes labelled X, Y and Z.

Index

numbers in italics refer to captions

Useful websites and further reading

AUTODESK
Free student licenses: plot stamp applied to AutoCAD;
AutoCAD/AutoCAD Architecture/3ds Max/ Maya /Revit
www.students.autodesk.com

Printed resources
McFarlane, B, *Beginning AutoCAD 2007,* Newnes Publishing, 2006
An excellent book based on the fundamentals of AutoCAD.

Matossian, M, *3ds Max 6 for Windows: Visual QuickStart Guide,*
Peachpit Press, 2004

The book gives a more indepth description of the basic tool
interface: a good intermediate book to develop your understanding
of 3Ds Max.

Robinson, M, *Maya 8 for Windows and Macintosh: Visual QuickStart
Guide,* Peachpit Press, 2007.

A good overview of the basic toolset and introduction to the
interface. Based on an earlier version, it avoids the many levels of
complexity that can be employed while using the program. A good
intermediate guide.

Website resources
www.cadtutor.net
CADTutor provides free video tutorials, articles, downloads
and a busy community forum for users of AutoCAD and
associated software.

www.cben.net
CAD Block Exchange Network: Online AutoCAD Block/Symbols
Library. CBEN is the largest, most comprehensive CAD library of
the internet.

http://wikihelp.autodesk.com/index.php?title=Revit/enu/2012/
Help/Revit_User's_Guide
Revit user guide, basic to advanced.

http://area.autodesk.com/
3ds Max and Maya tutorials and forum. If something has gone
wrong or you need to find out how to do something, a search on
the site will normally be fruitful.

SKETCHUP
(Trimble/Google) Basic version free: SketchUp Pro discounted
educational license.
www.sketchup.com

Website resources
http://support.google.com/sketchup/
A comprehensive guide to the SketchUp interface, suited to both
beginners and advanced students.

www.sketchup.google.com/3dwarehouse/
An extensive online collection and sharing site for SketchUp models

VECTORWORKS
Time-restricted free academic license/plot stamp
http://student.myvectorworks.net

Printed resources
Baer,T, Mcmillan, S, *VectorWorks 10 for Windows and Macintosh:
Visual QuickStart,* Peachpit Press, 2002

A dated but affordable book (most are quite pricey) to help you
develop your Vectorworks skills. Intermediate.

Website resources
www.vectorworks.net/training/free_resource.php

Tutorials based on the tools and the working methodology of
the program.

http://techboard.vectorworks.net/

Vectorworks community forum; good for troubleshooting.

Form Z 7
Trial or discounted 12 month academic license

www.formz.com

Website resources
www.formz.com/support/downloads/documentation.html

Very little has been published on Form Z that's up-to-date. The best
resources are the user guides as they are extensive and go into a
good level of detail.

www.formz.com/webinars/webinarReplay.html

Web video tutorials demonstrating the use of Form Z 7.

PHOTOSHOP
30 day trial – discounted educational version is still very expensive

www.adobe.com/uk/education/students.html

Printed resources:
Adobe Creative Team, *Adobe Photoshop CS6 Classroom in a Book.*
Pearson Education (US), 2012

So many Photoshop books are published that it would probably
take a book in itself to list them; a wise purchase would be the
official Photoshop manual.

Dernie, D., *Architectural Drawing,* Laurence King Publishing,
London, 2010

Some good Photoshop step-by-step guides.

Website resources
www.photoshop.com

Everything you need to learn Photoshop in one place.

General CAD-related reading

Dunn, N., *Architectural Modelmaking*, Laurence King, 2010

Hoverstadt, L., *Beyond the Grid: Architecture and Information Technology*, Birkhäuser, 2009

Iwamoto, L., *Digital Fabrications: Architectural and Material Techniques*, Princeton Architectural Press, 2009

Kolarevic, B. (ed.), *Architecture in the Digital Age: Design and Manufacturing,* Spon Press, 2003

Lunenfeld, P, *Snap to Grid*, MIT Press, 2001

McCullough, M, *Abstracting Craft: The Practiced Digital Hand*, MIT press, 1998

Picon, A, *Digital Culture in Architecture: An Introduction for the Design Professions*, Birkhäuser, 2010

Sennett, R., *The Craftsman*, Yale University Press, 2008

Picture credits

Except for the following, all the images in this book have been created by the author using CAD software programs. In all cases every effort has been made to credit the copyright holders, but should there be any omissions or errors the publisher would be pleased to insert the appropriate acknowledgment in any subsequent editions of this book.

p4 Becky Breed, No1 Pumphouse Arts Centre

p5 Jemma Greve, Swansea Bus Station redevelopment

p37 Silvija Meilunaite: plan and section for Contemporary Arts Centre

p10 Atelier Bow Wow House, the practice's office, by Yoshiharu Tsukamoto, Momoyo kaijima and Shun Takagi, Atelier Bow Wow

p60 (bottom image) Landscape Playhouse Project, 2001, laser-cut and 3D printed models by Achim Menges, photo © Achim Menges

p61 Jellyfish House project © IwamotoScott Architecture; proces2: Digital modelling and rendering consultant

p112 and p117 (below) Sarah Everitt, Pumphouse Basement View

p114 Gwanggyo Power Center © MVRDV; Pig City © MVRDV

p118 (above) Becky Breed, No1 Pumphouse Arts Centre; (right) Jemma Greve, Swansea Bus Station redevelopment

p168 Heidi Flanders, Cocktail Bar

p170 (below) Steph Glover, Gasometer Garden

p171 (left) photograph by Nicolas Grospierre, The Afterlife of Buildings. Metropolitan, 2008; (right) photomontage by Kobas Laksa, The Afterlife of Buildings, Metropolitan, 2008

p174 Steph Glover, Citysnooze Hostel

p175 Rendering by Sheena Roe

p177 Rebecca Groves, Crumlin Navigation Colliery, Public Farm, 2011

Author's acknowledgments

I have been wanting to write this book for some years and I owe thanks to the many students who have helped me understand the workings of computer-aided-design. By the subject's very nature, there is always something new to learn and there is always someone who will know more than yourself, do something differently or demonstrate a more time-efficient method. Having taught the subject for many years I can confidently say that it is the interaction with students in an educational environment that makes CAD such a rewarding subject to be involved in.

In the early days of my teaching, my family and my wife Sarah have born the brunt of my countless early mornings trying to get programs to perform correctly, and endless restarts from personal Frankenstein PC creations. It is with their support that I have been able to develop this specialism and they have further extended their support while I was writing this book.

I would like to thank Mike Fleetwood for encouraging me to teach differently, to lecture and prepare my program in a more progressive way. It was his analytical approach to the subject that helped me form a better academic understanding of the subject area. During my MA in Fine Art, Paul Bechaump encouraged me to work to my strengths and explore the potential of CAD in fine-art practice.

While writing this book I have had some very positive support from my department, Fashion and Retail, at the University of South Wales, for which I am very grateful. Tracy Pritchard has been very accommodating with the simple things in life such as rail fares and allowing me the space to write and research the book. I would also like to thank absent colleagues Jan and Richard.

Finally, and not least, I would like to thank Laurence King and the team I have been working with, particularly Philip Cooper, Gaynor Sermon and John Round. I have had some wonderful support and advice during the early development stages and while writing the book; the process has been engaging and I have learnt so much.